'BILL BLAIKIE'

LIEUTENANT COLONEL WILLIAM BLAIKIE, MNZM

BACK FROM THE BRINK

PTSD: THE HUMAN COST OF MILITARY SERVICE

Published by: William Blaikie, Upper Hutt, Wellington

ISBN: 978-0-473-42170-0
www.billblaikie.nz

If you are living with PTSD/PTSI and want information about Bill's Journey, articles, or some of the services he's found that might be of help to you or your family, please visit: **www.ptsdyouarenotalone.org.nz**

Dedicated to my darling wife Nancy, and our children.

Table of Contents

PTSD Explained

PTSD, or Post-Traumatic Stress Disorder, is a set of reactions that can occur after someone has been through a **traumatic event**. The chance of developing PTSD depends on the type of event experienced.

The main symptoms of PTSD are:

Re-living the traumatic event through distressing, unwanted memories, vivid nightmares and/or flashbacks. This can also include feeling very upset or having intense physical reactions such as heart palpitations or being unable to breathe when reminded of the traumatic event.

Avoiding reminders of the traumatic event, including activities, places, people, thoughts or feelings that bring back memories of the trauma.

Negative thoughts and feelings such as fear, anger, guilt, or feeling flat or numb a lot of the time. A person might blame themselves or others for what happened during or after the traumatic event, feel cut-off from friends and family, or lose interest in day-to-day activities.

Feeling wound-up. This might mean having trouble sleeping or concentrating, feeling angry or irritable, taking risks, being easily startled, and/or being constantly on the lookout for danger.

It is not unusual for people with PTSD to experience other mental health problems like depression or anxiety. Some people may develop a habit of using alcohol or drugs as a way of coping.[1]

PTSD v's PTSI

Post-Traumatic Stress Disorder (PTSD) is the medical term which is used worldwide and is the diagnosis and treatment term used by medical professionals and it is based on the Diagnostic and Statistical Manual of Mental Disorders (DSM). In 2013, the American Psychiatric Association revised the PTSD diagnostic criteria in the fifth edition of its Diagnostic and Statistical Manual of Mental Disorders (DSM-5; 1). PTSD is included in a new category in DSM-5, Trauma-and Stressor-Related Disorders. All of the conditions included in this classification require exposure to a traumatic or stressful event as a diagnostic criterion.[2]

In recent years the veteran community and many medical professionals have espoused that the term PTSD be changed to PTSI. With the recent rate of increase with suicides and incidences of PTSD being diagnosed among the veteran community, it has been a question of debate: whether changing the name post-traumatic stress disorder (PTSD) to post-traumatic stress injury (PTSI) would help reduce the stigma around the condition. Post-Traumatic Stress Disorder has been an accepted diagnosis since 1980. It's believed it is time to adopt a new name – Post-Traumatic Stress Injury. PTSI is more accurate, hopeful and honourable.[3]

---

[1]   2017 http://phoenixaustralia.org/recovery/effects-of-trauma/ptsd/

[2]   2017 https://www.ptsd.va.gov/professional PTSD-overview/dsm5_criteria_ptsd.asp

[3]   2017 http://globalptsifoundation.org/ptsd-vs-ptsi

Introduction

During my early childhood, I was brought up in Papua New Guinea where life is one big adventure. It was a place where kids could be kids, and it didn't matter what background you came from. These were the happy times, and I still look back at this period as being the most joyful part of my childhood. I was brought up to know right from wrong and that basically everybody had some good in them. It was a trusting environment. My later childhood was dominated by attending a boys-only private boarding school in Australia. It was there that I encountered strict discipline and the instilling of moral values that I still hold firmly today. I personally thrived in this environment; knowing where the boundaries were and the consequences of going beyond those boundaries.

It was also here that I was introduced to the military style of life, rising to achieve in my final year, the rank of Senior Army Cadet Officer and the prize for outstanding leadership. I knew by this stage of my life that my goal for my career was going to be an officer in the Australian Defence Force. I achieved this goal 1986 by graduating from the Australian Royal Military College, Duntroon in Canberra, Australia. It was here that my military career started in earnest and I was destined to become an Intelligence Officer in the Australian Army.

As a young man, I can look back and see that I was by no means a saint. I had my fair share of run ins with the law and was at times a little out of control. Perhaps subconsciously before I joined the military there was a fire in my belly that needed to be nurtured through parties and a bit of riotous activity before 'buckling down'. Much to my parents' relief, it didn't take too many years for me to settle into my adult life and career. However, I'm sure they had a few doubts at times, as I did about my direction for the future.

During the fifteen years that I spent in the Australian Defence Force (ADF), I was lucky enough to hold some very challenging intelligence positions. These jobs ranged from your typical Headquarters (HQ) intelligence staff officer positions to electronic warfare and counter-intelligence roles. I also served in a number of intelligence instructor positions and as the Executive Officer for the Australian Defence Intelligence Training Centre. While I really enjoyed my time there, for family reasons in 1999 I decided to leave the Australian Defence Force, and I moved to New Zealand with my then fiancé, Nancy to start a new life with our daughter leaving behind my two sons from a previous marriage.

After a short period of working in the private sector, I was approached by the New Zealand Defence Force (NZDF) to see if I'd be interested in joining the New Zealand Army as an Intelligence Officer. I thought long and hard about whether or not I wanted to resurrect my military career or continue working in the private sector. At the time the offer seemed too good to turn down, mainly because there were opportunities for operational deployments overseas. As with most individuals who join the military, the opportunity to put to the test those skills you had been learning and practicing in the peacetime environment was too good to resist. During this period the NZDF was expanding its commitment to conflicts overseas such as East Timor, Iraq and Afghanistan. Between 2001 and 2004 I held the position of Officer Commanding for the New Zealand Army Intelligence Company, followed by an appointment as the Intelligence Officer in the New Zealand Battalion Group, deployed to East Timor. Following this deployment, I was posted to the HQ Joint

Forces New Zealand (HQ JFNZ). While there I was selected to be the Military Assistant in support of the then Prime Minister Helen Clarke's during her visit to Afghanistan and Iraq in 2003. In January 2004, I was deployed to Afghanistan. It was this deployment that was going to have a life-changing effect on me for many years to come.

1

Bill's Story - Daily Life in Kabul

10:30 PM Kabul, Capital of Afghanistan

As the evening haze settles in on yet another stifling day in Kabul I return to my safe house. The pungent smell in the air irritates my nostrils, and I can taste the dust which is ever present in my mouth. The day is finally coming to an end after 16 hours at work. As I enter my safe house, I unload my rifle and pistol and remove my body armour, the relief of tension is immediate as I feel the weight of the day is finally starting to ease. I walk into the kitchen and grab myself some snacks from the US rations that are always there in abundance. On my way to my room, I say g'day to a few of the other occupants; we are all too exhausted for conversation.

I get into my room and look at the bed and think I could just collapse into it and go and sleep for a week. However, my day has still not ended. I log into my secure computer to check what messages I received from HQ JFNZ. There are a number of emails from my home HQ relating to the drudgery of administration which is the life of the Senior National Officer (SNO) for New Zealand in Kabul. I prioritise what needs to be dealt with straight away and what can wait. Then it dawns on me that tonight I'm required to write my weekly situational report back to New Zealand. This means yet another hour of work before I can finally rest. As midnight approaches I finally collapse into my bed, not even bothering to have a shower, and within minutes I am asleep. Sleep is easy to come by as I am exhausted at the end of each day.

In early 2004 I was posted to Afghanistan as the Deputy Director of Intelligence for Joint Forces Command - Afghanistan (CFC-A). The position I was taking up was a brand-new role for New Zealand as the CFC-A was only established in January 2004. Apart from my role as a Deputy Director Joint Intelligence, I also assumed two other national roles on behalf of the New Zealand Defence Force (NZDF) and the New Zealand Government:

1) I was the Senior National Officer (SNO) for all New Zealand troops posted within the Kabul area of operations. These included officers who were posted to the International Security Assistance Force (ISAF), New Zealand Army trainers and other staff within the Kabul region.

2) The other position which I occupied was that of the first New Zealand Defence Attaché posted to Kabul. This was more of a strategic role in support of the New Zealand Ministry of Foreign Affairs and the Ministry of Defence. As the Defence Attaché, I also acted on behalf of the New Zealand Ambassador to Afghanistan in his absence, as he was posted to Tehran and only visited Afghanistan on a six-weekly basis or when urgently required. On arrival in Kabul, I was instantly aware that the pressures and responsibilities would be immense and that to juggle these roles would be a challenge but not insurmountable.

The early morning call to prayers would always instantly bring me out of my exhausted sleep. The pressure of the day started from when I first opened my eyes; within half an hour I'd finished all my obligatory morning routine and headed off to work. On leaving the safe house once again, that pungent smell of smog and dust invaded my senses and brought me back to the reality that this was Kabul.

Donning my body armour before leaving the safe house, instantly reminded me of the pressures and weight of responsibility that I had not only on myself but on the soldiers under my command. Before leaving the safe house, the Afghan guards ensured that the area around the gate leading out to the street was clear and safe and then I would walk out of the safe house, acutely aware of everything that was going on around me.

The safe house I occupied in Kabul was by luck only situated 100metres down the road and across from the HQ compound so it was natural to get there by crossing the street and walking down the footpath. However, this was not as straightforward as it sounds. It was standard practice not to do this as individuals, and we normally waited at the gate of the safe house for one of two other personnel who were also going to the HQ, for much needed safety in numbers. I constantly felt like a giant 'head on a stick' trying to see anything out of the unusual - who was looking, windows the type and weight of the vehicles? (e.g. Being low on their springs could indicate a bomb, etc.).

Entering the compound was no different to any other complex or secure area in Afghanistan. It was a series of bollards and HESCO Bastions (Collapsible wire mesh containers with a heavy-duty lining filled with sand, soil or gravel). Once inside the corridor leading into the compound, there was an immense sense of relief as there were guard towers manned by US Soldiers overlooking the street and the corridor. Once I checked through a gate, by producing the security pass, the first order of the day was to unload my weapons. It was standard operating procedure, that once inside the HQ compound all weapons must be in the unloaded state. This was to prevent any accidental discharge and/or injury.

The first part of the morning over it was time for breakfast, not much I can say about that. As I was one of the few non-Americans posted to the HQ we had to succumb to the US diet or should I say the US Army food. The mess facility was manned by Afghan civilians who served breakfast which consisted of anything and everything fried, powdered eggs, and of course the obligatory cereal called Grits (food made from corn that is ground into a coarse meal and then boiled). This I can't recommend to anybody. I usually had breakfast with co-workers from around HQ and tried to introduce a bit of levity before the start of the actual work day.

With breakfast over I then headed over to my place of work which is what we called the Intelligence Directorate. This consisted of two houses within the compound. One house, later a purpose built containerised facility, was the Sensitive Compartmented Information Facility (SCIF; pronounced "skiff"). The other house was where our counterintelligence and human intelligence support element (2X Staff) [1] was located. These personnel were responsible for real-time, immediate human intelligence source work with the emphasis on identifying and locating High-Value Targets (HVT's). It was quite ironic to us when we found out that the house we had occupied for this purpose was previously the Iranian Ambassador's house before 2001.

The first task of the day for me was that my staff were required to give me a briefing at 7 a.m. every morning about the activities that had occurred overnight and anything that was planned for the next 24 hours. This detailed briefing meant that my senior staff and I were able to get a good grip on the operational situations we were dealing with. At the conclusion of the brief, it was my responsibility to pull out those parts of the intelligence picture which were required for a number of sensitive and high-level briefing documents that we produced first thing every morning. These briefing documents were for the Commander of CFC-A and other subordinate units as well as the US Ambassador to Afghanistan.

By 8 a.m. It was time for me to head over to the HQ morning conference, where the commander Lieutenant General David Barno would hold his morning brief. Present at the morning brief were all his senior commanders of the HQ, ranging from intelligence, operations through to planning, logistics information operations and civil affairs. This daily briefing was crucial as a means of setting the tempo for the day and also for future combat operations and redevelopment operations.

├─────┤

While this all sounds like a solid routine, for me each day brought different tasks and responsibilities apart from my primary job of being the Deputy Director of Intelligence and running the day-to-day function of the Intelligence Directorate. Returning to my office after the morning briefing I'd talk to my senior staff about future directions and requirements that were put on us. I then had to incorporate those other tasks that were part of the role as liaison between my directorate and the numerous other military government and NGO organisations.

This required me to do a lot of travel within the confines of Kabul to all the various agencies. To achieve this, it was necessary to move around Kabul in a manner that would attract the least amount of attention and yet provide me with adequate security and communications. As a result, I was given a civilian Toyota Landcruiser with blacked out windows and no military markings whatsoever. These types of vehicles were extremely numerous throughout all of Afghanistan - the idea was to blend into the environment as best you could and move around the city with a minimum of fuss and visibility. I also had two US Marines as my personal protection officers with me at all times, whenever I left the compound.

These two very young gentlemen turned out to be exceptional soldiers and also became good friends by the end of my tour, as we depended on each other. Sean and Jason[4] were already on their second tour of duty in Afghanistan. In their previous tours they had been on the front line in the battle against the Taliban and Al Qaeda. Their speciality was as scouts for a reconnaissance

---

[4]   Not their real names

unit. Jason and Sean were extremely professional soldiers, and we developed a very close relationship which is typical for small groups. It was imperative that you trusted and relied on each other when things became tough. Jason was the dominant one of the two and also senior, but only by a few months which got up Sean's goat. However, you could always rely on Sean to come out with a great one-liner that kept us entertained, and he brought some normality into the group. Humour was an essential part of maintaining some form of sanity in a city like Kabul that was full of danger and uncertainty.

Groundhog Day Doesn't Happen in a War Zone

As much as I wanted to plan out my day every morning, flexibility is always the first principle of warfare, because things changed rapidly and I had to react to those changes and be where I needed to be to carry out my duties.

As no two days were the same except the morning and evening routines, I was constantly on the go. I relished being in this ever-changing environment as I loved having to be mentally agile and always addressing new challenges. The set daily routine would kick in again around 7p.m. at night at with another briefing by my team in the Intelligence Directorate, outlining what had happened in the previous 12 hours, after which I would issue tasks for the next 24 hours.

The Intelligence Directorate was manned 24 hours a day as two shifts - day and night. After the evening brief, I always sat down with my senior section chiefs to discuss any issues they were having, the reallocation of tasks and on numerous occasions open brainstorming sessions to deal with the complex nature of counter insurgency warfare and redevelopment tasks. The nature of the environment in which we were operating was very fluid and pushed our mental agility to the extreme to try and solve complex problems that are inherent by the nature of the Afghanistan culture, society, psyche and history.

During each week I tried to allocate some self-time by going to the gym and working out - more to relax the mind than obtain any physical outcome. Because of the nature of my position, I just had to fit it in when I had downtime. Sundays were always a bit more relaxed than a typical working day however operations still continued and required that I carry out my routine briefing and running of the Directorate. I was never far away from work, to the extent I could not switch off for any considerable period of time. That is the nature of the beast while working in an operational area. The body becomes conditioned to survival mode and functions on adrenaline with very little sleep and for me constant mental awareness/alertness.

2

Building a Team

Lieutenant-General David Barno (USA)[5] was a man of average physical stature but this in no way depicted his tremendous strength in command and leadership. It was evident from my first meeting with him that he was a distinguished combat leader and had a real grasp of what was required to establish a counter insurgency campaign for Afghanistan. He was very approachable and liked to get to know his senior staff well. What I remember about my opening meeting with him was that he was glad that he had a Kiwi (slang term for a New Zealander) Officer serving as Acting Head of Intelligence. He stressed that I

---

5   General Barno was appointed to the rank of Lieutenant General in November 2003 at age 49, becoming the first member of his West Point class of 1976 to achieve that distinction. The previous month, he deployed to Afghanistan where he was designated to establish a three-star HQ in Kabul and ultimately command over 20,000 Coalition Forces for 19 months as the first Commander, Military Operations-Afghanistan (later redesignated Combined Forces Command-Afghanistan), United States Central Command. During his tenure, he forged a close relationship with U.S. Ambassador Zalmay Khalilzad, co-locating his command at the U.S. Embassy compound and creating an integrated civil-military counter-insurgency campaign plan for Afghanistan focused on the Afghan population. (http://rfpb.defense.gov/Board-Biographies/barno - 2017)

would have access to all US intelligence sources as he believed in the notion of a truly coalition HQ. He was open to frank discussions about where the campaign was heading and gave clear and unambiguous guidance. He was extremely personable, and we had many one-on-one discussions about my military background and my thoughts on the intelligence approach needed to support his campaign.

When I arrived in Kabul in early 2004, I was thrown into a fast-paced environment of establishing a new strategic HQ for Afghanistan. On top of this, I was to act as the Director of Intelligence for CFC-A as the American appointed Director would not be in the country for at least six to eight weeks. Upon arriving, my intelligence directorate consisted of only four individuals who immediately gave me confidence as they were senior in their roles, very experienced and most of all, very easy to get along with.

Initially there was little direction coming out of the command level structure of the new HQ, as it had only been operating for a few weeks. It dawned on me very quickly that *Lieutenant* General Barno was going to prove to be an exceptional commander and provide the leadership and guidance needed to build this HQ into a fully functioning strategic level command. The first order of business as commander, was that he needed to get a grip on all HQ staff and particularly the Heads of Directorates. As this was a new HQ and we were operating in an environment which was essentially counter-insurgency operations or otherwise described as COIN.[6] It became evident that there were significant discrepancies amongst the senior HQ staff as to how to operate in counter-insurgency operations.

---

[6]   According to the U.S. Government Counter Insurgency Guide (2009) counter-insurgency or counter insurgency (COIN) "may be defined as 'comprehensive civilian and military efforts taken to simultaneously defeat and contain insurgency and address its root causes "Insurgency is the organized use of subversion and violence to seize, nullify or challenge political control of a region. As such, it is primarily a political struggle, in which both sides use armed force to create space for their political, economic and influence activities to be effective."

Lieutenant General Barno then made it clear that his US Army staff at all levels had to quickly grasp the concept of counter-insurgency operations if we were going to be an effective HQ. The first couple of weeks were frantic in that HQ had to start commanding the subordinate units and producing plans as to how they would run the campaign plan. On top of that, it was identified early that the entire HQ was woefully undermanned to achieve the task it had been given. My role as Acting Director of Intelligence was to set in place a program to build an intelligence directorate that could support strategic level operations. This meant building a team that was capable of carrying out intelligence support for operations that covered the whole of Afghanistan.

CFC-A was established in November 2003 as combat operations in Afghanistan declined, and the focus shifted to stability, security and reconstruction. CFC-A was tasked with concentrating on political-military efforts, with responsibilities at the strategic level across Afghanistan, Pakistan, Tajikistan, and Uzbekistan. Continuing warfighting operations were the responsibility of the subordinate Combined Joint Task Force (CJTF-180 (US 82nd Airborne Division) until April 2004, when the task force was replaced with CJTF-76 (US 25th Infantry Division). The portfolio for CFC-A was extremely broad, and along with CJTF 180/76, oversaw the Office of Security Cooperation – Afghanistan (OSC-A) which was responsible for developing the Afghan security sector, both military and police. Without diving too deeply into the morass of US military organization, the challenge of CFC-A was that it was responsible for planning, coordination, and executing strategy at the highest level. This meant there was constant engagement with the US Embassy and its dynamic ambassador Zalmay Khalilzad, embassies and forces of partner nations and the Government of Afghanistan.

The Intelligence Directorate was responsible for providing intelligence support, analysis and targeting for strategic level operations in Afghanistan. As mentioned previously the Intelligence Directorate was also responsible for support to combat operations specifically on high-value targets HVT's, rogue war warlords, narcotics, and the complicated factional divide that makes up Afghanistan.

Added to this complicated matrix of requirements, I was told that I wasn't going to receive an intelligence unit as a whole entity to support this. Therefore, the dilemma was that I was required to build this organisation by gaining staff on a drip feed basis. By the end of my six-month deployment, I had built an intelligence directorate of some eighty plus personnel. What made the task more difficult was that staff had started to arrive from the US to fill the roles from a myriad of organisations and professional backgrounds.

It soon became apparent that there were two categories of individuals who were posted into the Intelligence Directorate. Firstly, were those professional intelligence operators who were career soldiers and the second category were made up of National Guard and Reserve personnel of varying qualifications ranging from academics and school teachers, to part-time intelligence professionals Hence this threw me a huge challenge as to how I was to employ each of these individuals to best suit their qualifications, rank and importantly the Intelligence Directorate requirements.

The difficulty was how to mould the team together to achieve all the tasks required and ensure the personnel mix was right so we could support all operations.

Mostly the organisation was broken down into the Counter-Intelligence (CI) and Human Intelligence (HUMINT) support elements and, the Intelligence Fusion Cell (IFC) which dealt with the regional analysis of day-to-day intelligence support for operations. Additionally to support the political arm of counter-insurgency operations, we established a cell dedicated to redevelopment tasks for the future growth for Afghanistan. On top of this already wide-ranging list of responsibilities, we also had to prepare for the first Afghan national elections since 1988.

Apart from running the day-to-day routine business of the Intelligence Directorate, one of my primary responsibilities was to ensure there were productive linkages between the intelligence directorate and external agencies including the myriad of US and allied intelligence and enforcement organisations, the leading agencies being the USA Central Intelligence Agency (CIA) and Drug Enforcement Agency (DEA). In the political spectrum, I was responsible for liaison between subordinate intelligence units and international organisations, such the United Nations Assistance Mission in Afghanistan (UNAMA) and a large number of NGO's, (Non-Government Organizations)

The roles and tasks that I was responsible for were diverse and for me extremely challenging and rewarding. I thrived in this environment in solving diverse and complex issues and ensuring that we provided the best service to the commander so he could achieve his mission. Every day was different and challenging, and this is what kept me engaged and focused, it was a constant adrenaline rush and incredibly satisfying. There was little time to reflect on anything, in particular, as we had to keep this 'beast' (intelligence support) moving forward and providing the results required. The situation in Afghanistan was complex, and extremely fluid which required me to ensure that the prioritisation of tasks within the Directorate was on the mark. The only things that remained constant were the daily briefing routines and my own command group meetings.

3

The Crux of the Matter

Testimonial – Captain Kevin Frank, United States Navy

Intelligence Director – Combined Forces Command – Afghanistan (2004-05)

"Lieutenant Colonel Blaikie's performance at Combined Forces Command –Afghanistan has been brilliant. He has guided the intelligence effort here to new areas that have substantially increased the effectiveness of intelligence operations in support of decision-making and combat operations. His ability to anticipate intelligence needs has been the critical element in the success of the Intelligence Directorate. No less impressive were his abilities to work with the international community and substantially increase both coordination and trust between Combined Forces Command-Afghanistan the United Nations and Non-Government Organisations. Lieutenant Colonel Blaikie was also able to successfully juggle the duties of Defence Attaché with those of Deputy Director Intelligence without degradation to either mission. Simply put, he can do it all well. He is the officer I want with me in combat.

LTC Blaikie demonstrated a level of competence in intelligence operations and analysis second to none in this HQ. On numerous occasions, his insightful and cogent analytical abilities were called upon to direct the execution of combat operations, as well as inform decisions from kinetic strike to reconstruction. His ability to mentor junior personnel in these matters was an added benefit, and greatly valued. His knowledge of technical intelligence is encyclopaedic, and his ability to transfer lessons learned from previous operations stood us in good stead, as we were able to avoid the pitfalls and key in on the important bits. His professional abilities were notable in all aspects of intelligence operations and especially useful in providing intelligence to planning and operation order development, as well as the design, organisation and manning of this operational HQ. He demonstrated a complete mastery of all aspects of intelligence."

⊢———⊣

One of the issues that became apparent early was that there was a lack of a common understanding regarding the security situation throughout Afghanistan. Seeing there was a significant gap in the intelligence picture throughout Afghanistan I established the Security Analysis Group (SAG). This forum comprised representatives from all organisations with security interests in Afghanistan. The formation of the group had a significant impact on improving information sharing and on situational awareness, as well as in operational planning and the subsequent execution of a wide variety of counterinsurgency activity, both kinetic, and in reconstruction and development.

At the weekly SAG conferences, my staff gave a general briefing on security situations covering the past week in Afghanistan and our concerns for the forthcoming week. Then, representatives of the other organisations would elaborate on what they had seen, heard, experienced through their own agencies regarding incidents and concerns that could add to the intelligence picture. This took an enormous amount of ground work on my behalf in convincing the military, UNAMA and non-government organisations (NGOs) to come together, put aside our differences (political, humanitarian and sociological) to share information to obtain a clear security picture of what was happening throughout Afghanistan. This was extremely helpful as a lot of the NGO's, and UNAMA were operating in areas throughout Afghanistan where there were no coalition forces or Afghan National Army. Therefore, our knowledge of what was happening in those areas was limited.

Thinking back on my tour of Afghanistan I rarely, if ever thought about the real pressure I was under, and I never stopped to smell the roses, and I mean that literally and figuratively. Kabul was known as the city of gardens and roses grew in abundance, thriving in the warm climate. There are stunningly beautiful gardens in compounds and Government enclosures; in particular, the Gardens of Babur in Kabul established in the 16th century, which is an oasis amongst the war rubble that makes up much of Kabul. Afghans have a long history for the love of gardening, however, during the Taliban era, this was not encouraged. Gardens were in abundance around our HQ but rarely did I stop to admire the beauty and colours. I suppose the primary reason is that I never thought about the pressure I was under. I just carried on and did the job at hand to the best of my ability.

I had been professionally trained as an officer at the Royal Military College Duntroon, Canberra, Australia and I was a professional career intelligence officer. My military training just kicked in, the job just had to be done. My training had instilled in me ethics and morals that are an essential fabric of what it means to be a professional officer. This, in particular, is one of the mental challenges I would face for many years after leaving Afghanistan.

Queens New Year's Honours 2005 – Member of New Zealand Order of Merit (M.N.Z.M.)

In January 2004 Lieutenant Colonel Blaikie was appointed to a senior staff position in the Combined Forces Command, Afghanistan, based in Kabul, as part of the New Zealand contribution to Operation Enduring Freedom. He played a significant role in guiding the Command's growing intelligence effort towards meeting the counterinsurgency threat and the redevelopment challenges. He displayed an excellent understanding of intelligence operations and the flexibility to discern what was important and how to adjust resources to do what needed to be done. He was instrumental in building the intelligence organisation from the ground up within the United States intelligence community and established the Security Analysis Group. This forum was set up by Lieutenant Colonel Blaikie on his own initiative and comprises representatives from all organisations with security interests in Afghanistan. The formation of the group has had a major impact on improving information sharing and on situational awareness, as well as in operational planning and the subsequent execution of a wide variety of counterinsurgency activity, both kinetic, and in reconstruction and development. Lieutenant General Barno, the US Army CFC - Combined Forces Command, Afghanistan has reported that in carrying out these very demanding duties, Lieutenant Colonel Blaikie demonstrated outstanding leadership and management abilities. He possesses the rare ability to analyse and soundly act upon even the most complicated challenges. He excelled in the austere conditions of Kabul, while working in a demanding forces environment.

4

Tension in Herat

In early spring of 2004, the build-up of the Afghan National Army (ANA) was continuing at a rapid rate. The aim was to extend the hand of the Afghani National Government and move forward toward unity. The idea behind this was to visually show the Afghan people that their country was on the road to establishing a national identity. This period in the emergence of the new Afghanistan was one of excitement and trepidation; no one knew where it would ultimately lead.

The western province of Herat was a relatively secure, autonomous sector under the control of a respected..... or feared.... warlord and governor, Ishmael Khan. Khan, also known as the Emir of Herat, had reasserted his power in the province after the fall of the Taliban. Once again Herat had become the transit hub for goods and supplies coming into Afghanistan from Iran and Turkmenistan. This had led to increasing tensions with the Afghan Transitional Administration as he refused to pass on to the government the revenues gained from customs' taxes on goods. This was a lucrative business as the majority of taxes went to Ismail Khan, not the national treasury. As governor of Herat, Ismail Kahn with the help of Iranian money had to rebuild the city since its destruction in the 1970's and 80's. Herat was also by far the most advanced metropolitan city in Afghanistan at that time, with uninterrupted electricity, water, and sanitation. There was even city garbage collection and street cleaning, which gave it the picture of a city almost untouched by war.

Maybe one of the biggest issues we in the West don't understand so well is that the tribal ways of those in the Middle East are arguably just as high functioning as they have been for centuries – just not the SAME as for us in the West. But then, what do we know?

├────────┤

Just before our arrival in Herat and the start of our mission, there had been a major incident that had claimed, among others, the life of the Aviation and Tourism Minister Mirwais Sadiq, who happened to be the son of Ismail Khan. Fighting had erupted in Herat between Ismail Khan's private army and the Defence Ministry's 4th Corps militia. Sadiq was killed by a rocket propelled grenade during the military standoff between his father's militia and the Defence Ministry's Herat 17th Division Commander, General Abdul Zaher Nayebzadah. The death toll from the fighting was estimated at fifty to one hundred people. The 17th Division HQ was overrun by Ismail Khan's private militia on 21 March 2004. The German Consulate was peppered with rocket propelled grenades and small arms fire, and the residents had to be evacuated to the U.S. Provincial Reconstruction Team (PRT).

In response to the fighting, 1,500 Afghan National Army (ANA) troops and their embedded U.S. advisors were to be deployed to Herat. The ANA was sent to the garrison of the 17th Herat Division of the Defence Ministry's 4th Corps, General Nayebzadah's HQ. The Afghan Government and the Coalition agreed that the deployment of an ANA force was imperative and essential, not only to the stability of the province, but also to show the extent of the National Government's reach. This was brought forward after the events of 21 March 04. One of the most effective ways to do this was to introduce the ANA in Herat province.

After the Sadiq incident, several high-level Afghan Government Officials were deployed to investigate. Concurrently, a small team of coalition personnel was selected to go to Herat to prepare the way for the ANA to move into the province. The team consisted of a U.S. Infantry Colonel, as Commander; a U.S. Army Operations Officer, a Major; and me as the Intelligence Officer. As tension built, the team felt excited that we were about to embark on a mission that was a real game changer in the Afghan rebirth. I personally felt a real sense of responsibility and pride that I had been chosen for this mission. For me to accompany the mission, I had to get clearance from the Commander of the HQ JFNZ in Wellington and the approval of the New Zealand Government, as this was outside my mandated mission. This was quick in coming, and our small team was assembled and prepared to leave. Before our departure, we received several briefings that set the tone for our mission.

One briefing was from the U.S. Ambassador Zalmay Mamozy Khalilzad, who left us in no doubt of the importance of this mission, not only to Afghanistan and the coalition forces in the country but to the wider international community and their continued support of the Afghan mission. This was to prove a significant advance for international relations and a win for international involvement in the War on Terror. It was anticipated that this mission would last only three to five days.

———

It was a lovely, crisp, spring day in Kabul as we assembled to drive to Bagram Airbase. We had just taken delivery of an 'up-armoured' Ford 4×4. I can remember that the doors were hefty to open and close, and the thickness of the windows was impressive; this vehicle would offer us some protection against a direct attack with heavy weapons or an IED (Improvised Explosive Device). It was a reassuring feeling to have such protection as we were not 100 percent sure of the reception we would receive on arrival in Herat. The reality of what we were about to embark on hit home and that knot tightened in my stomach as it invariably did when entering unknown areas of increased danger.

The drive out to Bagram Airbase in the early afternoon was uneventful. It was a well-travelled road by military vehicles as it was the main arterial road between the major air base and Kabul. On arrival, we met with operations and intelligence personnel members of Task Force 180 (Afghanistan Coalition Operational HQ) to get final briefings before we departed. I knew it was imperative that I absorb every detail of the mission since my judgments would be critical to a successful outcome.

Later that afternoon, we met the very experienced US Air National Guard C130 Hercules crew who were to fly us to Herat. We loaded our vehicle and stores which were destined for the U.S. Provincial Reconstruction Team (PRT) based in Herat.

We boarded the aircraft at around 10p.m. as our touch down window was around midnight. We were unaccompanied on our journey to Herat but were being tracked all the way by the multitude of air assets that operate 24/7 in the Afghan theatre of operations. Once the ramp of the C130 airplane closed, it dawned on the three of us that we were going into an unknown situation that had the option of turning pear-shaped at any time, given the unpredictable nature of Afghan politics and power struggles. As we settled down for our two-hour flight, longer than normal due to routing and tactical threats, we went over our mission. It would be a bit of "suck and see," as we didn't know what reaction we would get from Ismail Khan.

⊢——⊣

Flying over Afghanistan, I couldn't believe that there was so much turmoil happening on the ground. The blackout landscape beneath us varied in our transit to Herat from nothing but desert to lush and very fertile valleys. I still vividly recall the magnificence of the mountains on cloudless moonlight nights - simply intimidating but beautiful - surreal - when it's full of bad people. We knew that the majority of those valleys were being used to grow poppies that stuffed the coffers of local warlords and government officials.

Arrival time at Herat was set for midnight to ensure most people would be off the roads and we could make a relatively uneventful entry. We were to be met by members of the PRT and escorted to the safe haven of their base in central Herat. Descending into Herat was more eventful than expected, as the aircraft crew had difficulty in locating the Infra-Red (IR) lighting put down by the forces on the ground to illuminate the Herat Airfield. After we landed, we clambered aboard our armoured Ford vehicle and waited for the doors to open and the OK to drive the vehicle off. This was it. There was no turning back. The apprehension was electric as we knew so much was riding on us doing our mission with a successful outcome. There waiting on the tarmac for us was the contingent of the PRT and protection party.

In no time we were on the road into Herat. Part of the protection party were locals that had been hired by the PRT to guard the PRT base. Later it would come to our attention that our arrival was not so unannounced, as these guards were loyal to Ismail Khan. This would pose a larger issue later on in our deployment.

Driving through the streets of Herat, the first thing I noticed was the street lighting as we came close to the city, the tidiness, and the tree-lined avenues, all of which were in stark contrast to the environment we were used to in Kabul. The trip to the PRT was uneventful, and once there we made our greetings, conducted a briefing on our mission, and then retired for the night.

My first glimpse of Ismail Khan was when, from a distance, we witnessed the burial of his son at the Herat cemetery. It was a large event that was bristling with individuals carrying weapons. It wasn't a place for foreigners to be. The atmosphere was tense, and even from our vantage point, you could sense it could become volatile at any moment. Driving past the main Herat cemetery was awe-inspiring when you knew the recent, violent history of this place with the occupation of the Soviet Army and Taliban.

In early 1979 Ismail Khan was a Captain in the Afghan Army, based in the western city of Herat. At the beginning of March of that year, there was a protest in front of the Communist Governor's palace against the arrests and assassinations being carried out in the countryside. The governor's troops opened fire on the demonstrators, who proceeded to storm the palace and hunt down Soviet advisers. The Herat garrison mutinied and joined the revolt, with Ismail Khan and other officers distributing all available weapons to the insurgents. Hundreds of municipal workers and people not dressed in traditional Muslim clothes were murdered. A garrison of Soviet advisors was overtaken, and all of its inhabitants: Soviet advisors along with their wives and children were massacred. The mob put severed heads of the victims on sticks and paraded them through the city of Herat. The government led by Nur Mohammed Taraki responded, pulverising the city using Soviet supplied bombers and killing an estimated 24,000 citizens in less than a week.[7]

This event marked the opening salvo or discharge of artillery of the rebellion which led to the Soviet military intervention in Afghanistan in December 1979. Ismail Khan escaped to the countryside where he began to assemble a local rebel force.

The cemetery was marked by thousands of blue headstones reminiscent of scenes in movies and documentaries of Arlington or the Somme Cemeteries depicting acres of headstones. Off to

---

[7]   Ismail Khan, Herat, and Iranian Influence by Thomas H. Johnson, Strategic Insights, Volume III, Issue 7 (July 2004) Coll, Steve. Ghost Wars. pg 40. 2004, Penguin Books.

the rear of the Muslim cemetery were several large dirt mounds. These mounds represent the resting place of hundreds of Soviet soldiers, their wives, and children who were massacred by the Mujahedeen Commander, Ismail Khan.

5

Boiling Point

The days in Herat were spent arranging meetings with the Mayor, the Commander of the Local Militia Division, the Chief of police, and other senior players. Our meeting with Ismail Khan would have to wait until we had completed all these preparatory meetings. Visits with the local government, police and military commanders were numerous, as nothing was ever agreed to in the first encounter. The Commander of the Defence Ministry's 4th Corps militia was particularly glad to see us. Liaising with the Afghan Police was polite but incredibly tense as they saw their role as the provision of security for Herat. In their minds, the ANA had no role to play. The Chief of police, in particular, showed an aura of distrust and left me with a feeling that he would turn in a blink of an eye. There was yet another tightening of my stomach muscles. Negotiations were protracted and required a lot of persuasion.

It soon became apparent that our week-long mission would be extended, but we knew not by how much. Eventually, we met the Mayor and other city officials and had numerous visits, all of which were very courteous and always were accompanied by lots of tea and trays of almonds and pistachio nuts. We explained to the Mayor and other officials the nature of our visit and made it clear we were there to ensure the peaceful reception of the first ANA troops into the province.

Several days after our arrival, the ANA arrived via road in a large convoy. We met them at the Herat International Airfield. Our first mission was to find an area where the ANA could establish a base. Initially, the ANA moved into the garrison of the 17th Herat Division. This was short-lived for two reasons. Firstly, none of the Herat Officials or Ismail Khan wanted the ANA to occupy a base within the city proper. Secondly, the barracks were heavily mined and strewn with unexploded ordnance. You had to watch your footing wherever you went. It claimed one of our ANA soldiers, who was seriously injured by disturbing an unexploded ordnance. The absolute horror of that really brought home the unpredictable nature of operating in such an environment.

After a period of living in this highly toxic environment and after many negotiations, it was agreed that the ANA could establish a base on the outskirts of Herat, a site which was previously an agriculture college. We also decided that a portion of the ANA force could be stationed at the Herat International Airport. This again was a dangerous area as it contained thousands of unexploded ordnances dating back to the Soviet occupation of the 1980s; everything from 500-pound bombs and napalm to artillery and anti-aircraft shells, mines and mortars to small arms ammunition. United Nations demining teams had been clearing the area for several years and had only just scratched the surface. This was a situation not uncommon to most of Afghanistan.

Several days after the ANA arrived in Herat, it was finally agreed that ANA troops could patrol in the city proper. However, they had to be unarmed. We gained assurance from local officials and the police that no harm would come to the soldiers. The local people were happy to see the ANA presence as they had become weary of conflict. We accompanied some of these patrols, and it was refreshing to see the reception of the locals, and the relief on the ANA soldiers' faces, as they had not known what to expect. This all happened before we came to meet the man himself, Ismail Khan. Negotiations to this stage had been conducted through his intermediaries.

├────────┤

Ten days after our arrival, we finally had an audience with Khan. We approached his residence on the hill overlooking Herat, Takht-e Safar Resort, a palatial mansion that had spectacular views and gardens. There was even a large, swimming pool that had seen better days and was dark green with untreated algae. On arrival at the entrance to the residence, we were met by a large contingent of armed men, obliviously the "Praetorian Guard." The guard commander was officious and demanded that we hand over our weapons and body armour, for security reasons. It was at that moment our hearts raced, and the raw emotions of the unknown came to the fore.

We had become accustomed to the ways of life in Herat, and we never went anywhere without our weapons. We subsequently locked our weapons in our vehicle where at least we had control over them, and simply had to trust the ANA Commander's security detail to watch over everything. The site was one of a stand-off - Kahn's henchmen armed to the teeth and obviously veterans of several campaigns and our young ANA soldiers armed only with personal weapons. Our party of six men comprised of only we three from Kabul, the ANA Commander, his Intelligence Officer, and the Commander of the PRT.

We entered a large sitting room overlooking the pool and gardens. The room was full of various individuals, some unarmed-obviously Khan's hierarchy-and several heavily armed men. These armed individuals had those eyes that just stared straight through you; disconcerting, to say the least. They were obviously veterans of many conflicts, and they were not just there for show. We were instructed to sit together on a large couch and await the arrival of Ismail Khan.

After toing and froing of officials to a side room, Khan emerged as if making a grand entrance. We all stood out of courtesy and were duly introduced. The tension was electric, though we were able to keep our composure and not show our real feelings of fear and apprehension. But the ANA Commander was visibly nervous and scared as he knew Kahn's past track record, and they were also from different tribes. Khan directed his first question to our Colonel, as to why we were in Herat, stating that there was no need for a Coalition presence as things in Herat were under control. The Colonel responded that our presence there was to ensure him of our help with integrating the ANA into the province and to brief the PRT.

This was then followed by a conversation about the deployment of the ANA within the city and its surroundings. Khan had been instructed by President Karzai that the ANA were there to stay and that he was to help facilitate the ANA integration.

The conversation then turned to discussions between the ANA Commander and Khan (in Afghani), which we could see immediately became extremely heated, with Kahn having the upper hand. After some time, Khan ordered the ANA Commander out of the room, and they, along with several of the armed men, moved to a nearby side room where they continued to speak in their native tongue (Afghani Persian), leaving us to wonder what was actually being said. The conversation grew even more heated, and we could clearly hear a one-way tirade. As we later found out, Khan had also made a phone call to Karzai outlining his displeasure of the situation. As we were left to sit in the room while this was going on, the tension in the air rose, and the presence of the armed men became exceedingly intimidating.

This is when you feel you are in uncharted territory and that you have no control over the events that are about to unfold. This period of time perhaps lasted only 20– 30 minutes but felt like hours. Eventually, Khan and the ANA Commander re-entered the room, and it was evident that our man was distressed and totally belittled and intimidated. Tears flowed down his cheeks as he settled down next to me. He was openly shaking, and I felt his terror like a tangible energy emanating from him. The encounter ended abruptly without any firm commitments from Kahn.

When we left the residence and recovered our weapons and personal belongings, we all breathed a big sigh of relief. Just the fact we had back our body armour, weapons, and the security of our vehicle gave us a sense of control, even though we were totally outnumbered and outgunned. I had been holding my breath at some level for the entire time as the tension in the room had been so intense.

It wasn't until my exposure therapy in Sydney that I really acknowledge what I was feeling during this meeting. I had hidden my true feelings of dread. Only after reliving this event during exposure therapy, over and over again, did all my hidden memories of that meeting come to the surface. I was able to recall the absolute feeling of total vulnerability and that my life was in the hands of someone else and I had no control. That memory of the tightness in my guts and the sweat beading on my forehead, to my sweaty palms is what I now feel every time I have to deal with an authority figures and in situations where I perceive I have no control.

⊢———⊣

Tensions were still high between followers of the local Divisional Commander and those loyal to Khan. After a period of about two weeks in the city, rumours spread that there might be a skirmish between these two groups. Caught up in all of this was the local United Nations mission, which had been in Herat for some time. It was decided that contingency plans needed to be made to evacuate the United Nations personnel to the PRT compound and to establish a defensive area around it. This was to prove almost impossible as the PRT compound was in the city centre proper and surrounded by civilian houses. A built-up area is not a desirable place to establish a defensive perimeter. To add to the mix was the fact Khan knew exactly what we were doing as the local guard force hired by the PRT was supplied by Khan and reported to him

As the tensions rose and word filtered in that there was possible trouble brewing, it was decided to enact our defensive plan in case of incursion by local forces loyal to Khan. It was rumoured that local mujahideen had armed themselves and would overrun the United Nations compound and rid the city of troops loyal to the local Divisional Commander. The situation was growing ever more tense and unpredictable. The Colonel in command of our mission took charge of the defensive operation of the PRT compound as the PRT Commander was ill-equipped with the necessary military skills.

While the Colonel and Major ran the command post with other PRT HQ staff, I moved to the roof of the central building in the compound as this provided an excellent vantage point to observe beyond the perimeter of the base. On the roof, a Special Forces Civil Affairs Team had set up satellite communications configured to talk to the air assets on standby. From here I was able to direct air assets overhead and instructed them to make a show of force by crisscrossing the city at low altitude. The use of a show of force in this instance was to have Coalition attack aircraft buzz the city at a low level indicating their presence and lethal weaponry. This proved most effective as the crowds dissipated. Militants and the Afghan population are all too familiar with the lethal strike power of coalition air assets.

This was the real deal as we knew we had to be on our game, and years of professional soldiering came to the forefront in what we call the "automatic mode" switched on. However, I could still feel the extreme tension and vulnerability, but overcame that by concentrating on the task at hand. As this situation evolved, an emergency response team was placed on standby in Kandahar by air; fortunately they were not needed.

The ANA was on the other side of the city, bunkered down in their temporary base with their U.S. advisors. They were in no place or state to offer us any real help, as they were a relatively new force. Khan's men, on the other hand, were seasoned fighters.

Tensions subsided in the city over the next couple of days, and things returned to relative calm. Our days had come to an end in Herat as our job was done. We had achieved the first major deployment of the ANA into a province and with it the extended authority of the Afghan National Government. Our mission had been a success. It had taken far longer than first expected, and the personal toll would not manifest itself until much later.

This was one of the several traumatic events in my tour of Afghanistan that year, and it has remained with me ever since. I now suffer from claustrophobia whenever I am enclosed in small spaces, and I struggle with the feeling of utter vulnerability whenever I am not in control of a situation. The hyper arousal is still with me today and manifests itself in many different ways daily. It was the constant tension and unpredictability of the whole situation I found myself in, but the meeting with Khan was the culminating point. I coped with the stress at the time by just putting all the incidents into that black box in the back of my brain, trying instead to concentrate on the immediate tasks ahead. All the time not knowing that this extended period of stress, tension, and the unknown would have a devastating effect on me years later.

6

Frozen in Time

The morning started out like every other morning in Kabul. But on this particular day, I was scheduled to have a meeting at one of the UN compounds across the city, which of course meant planning our journey using the safest route, checking out the radios, which were vital for communications and safety when traveling around Kabul, as well as having a mission briefing with my Marine guards Sean and Jason. As usual, I filed the task with our operations staff. This is done so they can track our movements through regular radio checks, knowing the schedule and routes we were going to take. I had been trained around the approach given to driving in a threat environment - continuously assessing where the threat may come from. Looking for escape routes, leaving gaps so you aren't blocked in, keeping the vehicle moving, not stopping for pedestrians who may be deliberating trying to get you to stop, using the horn and weapons to forecast your intent.

While this routine was no different to the countless times we have gone through this process, this day's events would have a dramatic effect on my personal well-being many years later.

I was driving with Sean in the passenger seat and Jason sitting behind me on the driver's side. As we left the security of the HQ compound, we entered the madness of what is Kabul traffic. Cars, trucks, motorbikes all vied for position on the dust ravaged roads with complete disregard for any road markings or road rules.

Approaching one of the many crowded major intersections, we found ourselves stuck in a traffic jam. Nothing was moving in any direction, but it did give us extra time to observe our surrounding environment - always on the lookout for threats and escape routes. While it's not unusual to get caught up in such traffic jams when travelling incognito, the hyper vigilance kicks in as soon as you're stopped due to the very nature of having to be extra aware of issues such as suicide bombers who were a genuine threat to everyday life at that time.

To our front right were a couple of local police cradling their AK-47s in a semi-relaxed fashion, not taking any particular interest in the situation. There were people everywhere, moving about through and besides the traffic – footpaths on the street being almost non-existent in the way we think of them in the West. I quickly noticed an individual in a burqa approached the vehicle from the front. She was moving at a steady pace towards us looking into each car she passed, but not pausing. From several car-lengths away she drew near to my side of our vehicle within a couple of minutes.

My hypervigilance was reaching epic levels as I knew the enemy had quite often used suicide bombers disguised in traditional burqas to get as close as they could to their intended targets. This individual then approached the front of our land cruiser and came to my window, just as she had to the previous vehicles she passed, but suddenly her movements of the past few minutes changed as she hesitated and placed her face up against my window to look inside the vehicle. Sean, Jason and I were on a knife's edge, as her hand came out from under the burqa and gestured towards me. Instantly I noticed that the hand was quite large with stunted fingers like a man's hand.

54

You know how things can slow down to split second by split second detail as something unfolds before you, that is threatening in nature? Whether a car accident or a child hovering about to fall from a high position that you know you might not reach to catch in time. As that hand reached up to gesture to us inside the car, her (or was it his?) dark eyes met mine through the netted veil of the burqa and the tinted glass, I felt fear in the pit of my stomach as did the highly-trained bodyguards I was travelling with. Time stopped, and the silence was extreme before our respective years of military training came to the forefront – years preparing for just such a moment as this.

The threat level at that moment in the car went through the roof. Sean sitting in the passage seat raised his weapon up and pointed it at the individual. I was suddenly acutely aware that the barrel of his gun was in line with my left ear. Jason in the back seat had his weapon pointing at the individual and only inches from my right ear. The Marines were yelling; "Should I shoot, should we shoot?" At this point, I yelled, "Don't shoot!" My mind was racing, and I wasn't aware that I was actually going through a risk assessment process and thinking about our options at such a warp speed that James T Kirk's head would have been spinning.

I quickly calculated there were three choices. Do nothing and hope the individual walked away. The second option was to do nothing and let the Marines open up. The third was for me to take aggressive action and shoot the individual. The Afghan policemen over to our right with their weapons were unaware of what was unfolding, we had absolutely no idea (or any confidence) in whether they would support our initiative or whether they would fire at us in instant retaliation, and so we had to treat them as hostile. However, given the circumstances of the tight traffic jam, being stuck and not moving, hundreds of people around and there was no way of escaping the situation. We were frozen in that moment!

There really was only one other option, and I made my decision quickly. My Sig Sauer pistol had been resting between my legs on my lap, and I grabbed it and raised the pistol to the window and pointed the barrel at the individual's head, knowing full well that it was already loaded and the safety catch off. I gestured and yelled at them to move on. I knew full well that if I had to take the shot, then all three of us would have been at the mercy of the crowd and that would not end well for us. Finally, he or she lowered their hand, broke their stare from mine to take one last glance into the car and then moved back towards the rear of the vehicle.

I watched in the side mirror walk as she (or he? I would never know) slowly made her way down to the back of our Landcruiser, pass the vehicle behind us and then disappeared into the melee. Three of us were in a state of shock and massive hyper arousal; scanning everything, everywhere, just to make sure that we were safe. We sat there for what seemed like an eternity not speaking but acutely aware of our surroundings.

The traffic jam eventually eased as quickly as it had built up, and I can't remember how many minutes later we moved on through the intersection and then onto our first call of the day. I recall getting to a secure compound securing our weapons holstering my pistol, leaving my long gun and body armour with the boys and going to my meeting. By this time my mind had moved on to this meeting, as it was important. So I just simply stored what had just happened away in the back of my mind.

It wasn't until the boys and I got back to our own compound after a very tense trip back that we thought about the incident again. On returning to the Intelligence cell several hours later we secured our weapons, and I grabbed a Coke and cigarette. I spoke to my Gunny (Marine Gunnery Sergeant) and a few others about the incident we had just being through. When we talked, it wasn't about the decision-making, wasn't about the fright, the fear or the terror. I was joking and laughing with Sean and Jason that if they had fired their weapons next to my ear, I would be bloody deaf, which ironically in that second of extreme tension was one of the other thoughts racing through my mind. It was all bit of a joke, and we dealt with it using black humour. Not long after that, the incident faded into oblivion along with a lot of other memories of my tour in Afghanistan. We continued to do a lot of travel around Kabul as my job required it of me. I know that each time we left the security of the HQ compound, we were extremely vigilant of our surroundings – more so than ever before. That hypervigilant feeling has never left me to this day! As soldiers, we minimise these incidents and use humour to mask our anxiety.

Today I can recall this quite vividly and picture it almost as if it was like a video. The clarity of the incident has come back in full technicolour with surround sound. This has led to me questioning every decision as if it has a life-and-death ring to it. I have to figure out why my brain has been holding onto the split second of the incident and not the whole episode. That split-second when I held my loaded pistol at someone's head and made that call not to fire (or not to kill someone!).

├────┤

I felt extremely tired at the end of my tour to Afghanistan, feeling myself to be in a state of perpetual risk-management. I believe our internal pendulums are off-centre when we get out of the threat environment, and they stay that way unless we have the support and environment in place to enable any moderating.

While dealing with my PTSD, professionals I've met with have reasoned that my ability to make that immediate and calculated risk assessment is the reason that my boys and I are still here today. I now have to figure out how this still affects me making decisions currently with my family. And how this has negatively and positively affected my work in the corporate/ private sector through the year's post-Afghanistan? Ultimately, I need to work through how I can overcome my indecision and lack of confidence?

7

Dislocation of Expectations

The Emirates airline flight arrived at Kuala Lumpur International Airport on a very balmy tropical morning. As I readied myself to the depart the aircraft, it dawned on me that over the last eight hours I had overindulged in fine wine and spirits. To put it bluntly, I was drunk! I can remember my backpack was heavy as I walked off the aircraft and all I could hear was the jingle of full miniature spirits bottles which I had pinched from the drink cart. After conducting the formalities of clearing customs and collecting my bag, I walked into the arrivals hall, and to Nancy my wife's bewilderment, I walked straight past her. In anticipation of my mid-tour break and our holiday in Malaysia together, Nancy had been exercising. She'd lost quite a lot of weight and with a totally new hair style was looking drop dead gorgeous! Unfortunately, in my inebriated state I nearly blew our first reunion.

This is how I started my mid-tour break; in a haze of alcohol trying to wash away the memories of the last few months of life in Afghanistan. Nancy, on the other hand, had been waiting for this moment for months, planning our beautiful holiday on the island of Penang in Malaysia. She had been looking forward to this moment, and here I was totally letting her down. The moment couldn't have been more different for the two of us. Me in complete avoidance mode and Nancy bubbling with excitement and expectations of an enjoyable holiday. This is how I started my mid-tour leave from Afghanistan.

The taxi ride from the airport to the Kuala Lumpur city seemed to take forever, and I recall that not a lot was said between us. However, I finally realised the situation I had created for Nancy and myself. Looking back in hindsight, I can still feel the tightness in my gut about the guilt of having let Nancy down when what she deserved was completely the opposite. Finally, we got to our hotel where I collapsed on the bed and slept for the next eight hours. On waking up and having wasted the first day of the little time we had together I committed myself to try to forget about Afghanistan and purposely not talk about it for the rest of the holiday.

The next day we arrived at our resort on Penang Island, we settled down to making the most of our holiday and just enjoying the precious time we had together. It was lovely to have time for lazing on the beach, shopping and just taking in the culture. We even spent a day hiring motorbikes and rode around the entire island experiencing the beautiful countryside and the bustling madness that is common to most Asian cities. I often still think about how one day you can be in the country that is tearing itself apart in conflict and then within 48 hours you can be in another country where the biggest danger is falling off a motorbike, while enjoying a ride through the countryside.

During our time in Malaysia, we wanted to experience as much of the local culture, cuisine and atmosphere as we could. One of the things we did every night was to go to restaurants that were mainly visited by locals, as we always knew the food would be good. These restaurants were busy, loud and crowded and the soldier in me was always looking for that table in the corner mapping, out where the exits were just in case something happened, and we needed to get ourselves out of there to somewhere safe. These days I am able to look back in hindsight and relate that feeling of having to know where the safety zone was, right back to my experience in Kabul where I was trapped in the traffic jam. So subconsciously my training and experiences had me always trying to keep Nancy and myself safe. While there were many local women wearing hijabs to cover their hair, due to Malaysia being mostly a Muslim country, this both helped and hindered my ability to relax. The sight of so many brightly covered heads in a peaceful country was in stark contrast to so many dark covered heads of women wearing more subtle or dark colours in Afghanistan. The women there working hard not to draw attention to themselves due to the dangers and conflicts that lurked everywhere.

One day, Nancy and I decided to hop on a local bus to ride into the city from our resort for some light shopping. It didn't take long for the smell of the diesel, the press of the people all vying for space to sit or stand, the heat and the Asian fragrance of dust and spices to create a feeling in me of desperately wanting to escape. I was inwardly terrified of being there and felt this incredibly strong urge to get my wife and me to safety – where that was I didn't know, but it was surely anywhere other than on that bus. I fought those feelings and tried hard to just breathe through it. I didn't want to alarm Nancy, but I was fighting a war inside myself that was fiercely provocative of all the anxiety I'd unwittingly brought with me from Afghanistan.

I presume this experience of dislocation of expectations is common among those people who one day find themselves in an environment which is harsh and threatening and then the next day in an atmosphere which is warm and welcoming. During the time of my break in Malaysia, I mentally tried to divorce myself from my experiences over the previous months and just concentrate on enjoying the moment in time with Nancy. Not knowing then that in years to come, I would employ the same methods of avoidance because of the dark times in Afghanistan which eventually had a severe effect not only on my life but the life of my family.

8

Leaving the Army

I returned from Afghanistan in August 2004 and soon after that my life, confidence and trust in others started to fall apart. I had had indications from the New Zealand Army that when I returned to New Zealand, I would be moving into the position of the Senior Intelligence Officer at HQ Joint Forces New Zealand (HQ JFNZ). However, it soon became evident that the New Zealand Army had different plans for my future. Instead, they wanted me to take a role in personnel branch to diversify my management skills.

Throughout my entire professional Army Officer career, I had been a specialist intelligence officer, and there were never any plans for me to be other than that. A move into personnel management was not at all where I had envisioned my career path taking me.

Looking back at that period, there is a lingering feeling of anger and bitterness. I felt dismayed that I would have to give up my speciality profession as an Intelligence Officer to do something I had no interest in. My experience over the last fifteen years and in particular my time as a Deputy Director of

Intelligence in Kabul, had me at the top of my game and career as an intelligence officer.

Let me explain further. The profession of Intelligence requires a sound knowledge of the intelligence systems and processes. During these early years of the war on terror, intelligence systems and processes were evolving rapidly and becoming more and more sophisticated. Therefore the skills quickly became perishable if you moved out of the profession. I had never been given any indication that my work in this field was anything less than extremely valued and of superior quality, and this all came as quite a shock to find my career path being derailed. I'm sure it's not unlike anyone working in any other industry, where you are made to feel powerless over the decisions made by senior management, who have a vision that does not necessarily align with the goals and ambitions of their key people.

I believe this is where my anger and disappointment and lack of trust of organisations to look after my interests started to creep in. I had developed and honed my professional skills to a very high level, and basically, I was asked to put all this on hold. I knew from my experiences and that of others over these past years that if you left the profession, it would be tough to come back into it and take up where you left off, as things were changing so rapidly.

Because I had this feeling of mixed emotions about my future career in the Army, and more importantly, my brain was still working in overdrive. All the time looking for threats so as a result of that I became sceptical of authority. Another area of concern which is now only understood with the benefit of hindsight and discussions with other army personnel, is that it is tough to come out of an operational area and simulate back into "normal" working and personal life – society!

This is in part why I am sharing my own story. The issues faced by many soldiers who have emerged back into society after spending a long time in high-pressure war zones – and arguably to some degree in peacekeeping zones too – is that understanding the time and support required to 'decompress' is still a relatively new science.

This is nothing new considering what our previous generations experienced post the great wars of the 20th Century. War trauma, shell shock or as it is now known, PTSD became more widely acknowledged officially over the past forty years since the Vietnam War.

This issue of assimilating back into a peacetime lifestyle is to me the heart of the matter of my own demise and also of anyone past and present who are deployed on military operations.

Therefore, I decided that for me it was best to leave the Army and pursue a career in the private sector. The decision to leave was not easy, but I felt I had to make this move so I personally could leave knowing that I had reached the pinnacle of my career as an Intelligence Officer. The feeling of anger and disappointment still haunts me today, and many emotions are running through my head at the moment as I write this. I also wonder for the millionth time if I had taken the advice of the Army and changed my career path and remained in the military family, would my life have taken a different turn and not the path that I'm on now.

This mixture of emotions and regrets is constant. It sends me into a sense of insecurity and lack of confidence in that did I make the right decision in leaving the Army? I know I can't change the past, but it still doesn't mean I don't think about the "What if?" I have a quote on my wall of my office that in some way helps bring me back to the moment. "The more you live in the past, the less of the future you have to enjoy".

Deciding to leave the Army was made even harder because on one hand elements of the Army were telling me that this change was good for me and good for the New Zealand Defence Force. On the contrary, my Commanding General at the time was telling me that he wanted me to stay and use my skills and that he couldn't see the rationale for the Army wanting to do what they proposed. This just added to my confusion and anger.

During this early period of my return from Afghanistan in 2005, I didn't think a lot about any of the particular situations I had found myself in. I was more preoccupied with trying to make day-to-day decisions that were rational for anybody in normal society, however, unbeknown to me each of these decisions were interpreted by myself as life and death decisions and could have dire outcomes. Every decision became awefulizing in that I had irrational and dramatic thought patterns, predicting the most catastrophic outcome in every circumstance. I was effectively mentally stuck in the role of a senior intelligence officer.

It wasn't long until Nancy noticed a real change in my behaviour and outlook. I would keep to myself and spent less and less time at home and with the family and more time turning to alcohol and hiding away in my own self-destructive cocoon. The rationale of being on my own and in my own bubble was that as long as I was by myself, no harm could come to my family and the people around me that I loved. The time we did spend together I was non-communicative and often angry and short-tempered for no particular reason.

Finally, one-day things came to a frightening head. My oldest son and I were in the kitchen, and he questioned one of my decisions in such a way as only a young teenage boy can. I suddenly grabbed him by the neck and not knowing my own strength lifted him off the ground and looked him straight in the eyes as my anger came up through me like waves crashing on a stormy beach. Within a split second, I realised what I had done and dropped him to the floor. I can't even readily recall what the discussion was about. What I do know was that he was questioning my judgement and I flipped straight back into that life-and-death mode where everything had extreme consequences. After realising what I'd just done, I ran outside to the garage and sat in there for hours sobbing my heart out. This was the one and only time that I have expressed my anger physically towards anyone in the family.

At a few other times, I had certainly experienced harsh shockwaves of anger, but I'd become adept at directing those outbursts into harming the walls or objects I could throw.

As weird as it may sound, I reasoned with myself that if I was only physically hurting myself - and yeah, bruised knuckles really do hurt like hell when they meet solid objects, regardless of how Schwarzenegger makes it look on the movies - then I wouldn't be hurting my family. This was one way of expressing my feelings and especially my guilt. The guilt being compounded every time I felt anger and took it out my family and myself. Looking back this is the period when my life and our family life started to spiral into some very dark places.

To add to the confusion, in December 2004, I was informed that I was to receive the New Zealand Order of Merit (MNZM) in the 2005 Queen's New Year Honours list. This recognition was bestowed on me for my services during my tour in Afghanistan against the War on Terror. Here I was being commended for my intelligence work on operations yet in my mind the Army was saying "Thanks, but we don't need your skills."

This was an incredibly difficult period of my life. I personally was so proud of myself for being recognised in this way. However, on the other hand, I felt immense guilt, that I didn't deserve this as not all operations in Afghanistan had gone to plan, and I was harbouring doubts about decisions I had made and in situations I had found myself.

9

Recognition for an Anxiety Riddled Hero

And so it was that on a wet and windy Wellington day on the 31st of March 2005, I took my family to Government House, where I received my Member of the New Zealand Order of Merit for services to the war on terror. While it was a proud moment for me and especially my family, I harboured some thoughts to myself that maybe I wasn't as deserving of this honour as others in the room that day. People such as Olympians, Emergency Service Personnel and extraordinary community minded people.

A few days before this, my father had arrived from Australia to attend this momentous occasion. When dad arrived in New Zealand, he kept telling me how immensely proud he was that his son was going to receive such an honour. I remember dad's constant questions about the work that I had done in Afghanistan and what I had achieved. This constant questioning by my father made me upset and angry to the extent where both he and I had some huge arguments over nothing at all. Dad had always been immensely proud of what I'd achieved in my military service, and at times throughout my life, I also gained the impression that maybe he was trying to live a bit of his life through my achievements. He had always talked of his own regrets in not joining the military when he was a young man after World War II. The dream he'd never realised had been to join the air force and fly aircraft. Before the day arrived for us to go to Government House, there was a lot of tension at home. I found myself anxious, and I would snap for no reason at all. Looking back in hindsight I was conflicted about receiving this honour because on the one hand, I was proud of my achievements and then on the other, I doubted myself as to whether I really deserved it.

The night before, I prepared my uniform, checking that everything was in order so I was ready to go the next morning. I had mixed emotions and was extremely anxious. Even when I woke up on that morning, I went through the motions of double-checking my uniform to make sure I was fully prepared to attend Government House. However, no matter how many times I checked and double checked that my uniform was in order so I would look as smart as possible; I had managed to overlook the important detail of attaching my Intelligence Corps badges to the collar of my uniform.

I had gone through this routine many times over the last twenty years and never have I failed to miss such an important detail on my dress uniform. It had become second nature to me, and I still wonder to this day how I managed to miss something that even a raw recruit wouldn't do.

Arriving at Government House, I was still extremely anxious and still hadn't realised that I'd missed this important detail on my uniform. All the intended recipients were ushered into a waiting room, where family and friends were seated in the main hall of Government House. While waiting for the ceremony to begin I chatted with other military people, and even they didn't seem to notice, that I was missing my badges, or maybe they were unwilling to let me know at this stage that I was incorrectly dressed. This small detail of missing my Corps badges on my uniform has even to this day caused embarrassment to myself to such an extent that I have never shown my ceremony photographs to anyone but my family.

Waiting for the ceremony to begin I looked around the room and was in awe, I was in the presence of some truly remarkable people from all walks of life and occupations. Some individuals were recognisable straight away as they were prominent public figures. One thing that sticks in my mind about that day is that I was among individuals who had done extraordinary things, committed extraordinary acts of bravery and reached the pinnacle on their own chosen professions. I remember meeting many gold-medal Olympians that day who had achieved remarkable feats. I saw all these other individuals as heroes in their own right, and I asked myself internally whether or not I was as deserving as they were.

After the ceremony, all the recipients and guests mingled over morning tea. My family and I took this opportunity to introduce ourselves to the high-profile Olympians that our children were in awe of. Looking back, I know I outwardly displayed the persona of a proud individual however, internally I felt incredibly lonely. This is one of the main traits of a person who suffers from PTSD; we are great actors who can openly portray one thing but internally feel another.

After the ceremony, my father took the family out for a celebratory lunch and reflected on what I had just achieved. However, the excitement over lunch was all about who we had the privilege of meeting and mixing with at Government House and enjoying their achievements. The rest of the day is a bit of a blur as I remember going for a drink and all I could think about was how stupid I must have looked in my uniform, without my collar badges when I was supposed to be portraying a professional army officer of the highest standard.

⊢——⊣

This feeling of being not as deserving as others and the burden of guilt stayed with me until 2016. It was during my month-long PTSD treatment in Sydney, Australia in 2016 that I finally found the compassion within myself to recognise that I had done some good in Afghanistan and should wear my medals with pride. It was during this treatment phase that my fellow group members, after hearing my trauma episodes expressed to me that I had made correct decisions which far outweighed any decisions or actions that didn't always turn out as well. Also while catching up with a close friend and Duntroon classmate after the course he told me - "It was always about you, not the uniform - you could have gone there in your pj's". It was also here that I started to realise that not everything has a rosy outcome, but you should enjoy all the good things that you have in your life and most importantly your family and those you love.

10

A Gradual Decline into Darkness

The period between 2005 and 2012 saw my own decline from being a highly regarded professional Army Officer to a shattered, broken man. I knew in 2005 when I left the army I was starting to have major issues with my personality and confidence. Once I decided to exit the Army, I chose to seek employment in which I could use my professional intelligence and management skills. As I had no other skills to fall back on, my employment options were limited. I sought out jobs that played to my strengths and would hide my weaknesses.

During this six-year period, I held four high-profile positions, all of which required me to work with small teams. In three of these teams, I was the manager and required to set direction and oversee them. These roles all fell into my comfort zone where all I had to worry about was myself and the small number of people around me.

These jobs included:

- New Zealand National Manager for Maritime Security.
- Senior Associate with a USA based consulting firm.

- Manager of Operational Processes with the New Zealand government personal accident insurer.
- Director of Strategy with the Royal New Zealand Air Force (RNZAF).

The common thread of these positions was that each was a newly established position requiring me to form a strategy and then implement that plan. This modus operandi was bread and butter for me, which enabled me to stay in my comfort zone.

Reflecting back on this period I can see that I averaged periods of 18 months to two years in each job. This was no means by design, but just good fortune. In all these situations, I threw myself into my work as I knew I had major deadlines to meet to implement individual strategies. This was somewhat easy for me to manage as there were set boundaries. However as each of the 18 month periods came and went I started to lose interest and focus. It was as if I had achieved the desired outcome and was ready to move on. In reality what was really happening was;I was throwing myself into my work, not to achieve the desired results but to take me away from the family unit, and the responsibilities that went with that.

Once these jobs became mundane, I had to turn to something else to distract my time and to keep me away from my family, so I didn't disrupt them, at least that was my thinking. So the pattern started to emerge that after about 18 months I would start to neglect my work obligations and turn to alcohol and the social scene that goes with it to occupy my time.

It was during 2006 and my first spiral into the darkness that Nancy convinced me to get some help to manage my anxiety and depression. I contacted the New Zealand Veterans Affairs (VANZ) and they sent me for a formal assessment with a psychiatrist. This evaluation established I had PTSD, Alcohol Dependence Disorder and a Major Depressive Disorder. The outcome was initially quite frightening.

However, I personally thought it wasn't that bad. I went along with their recommendations and started to attend counselling with a clinical psychologist and also went on antidepressant medication. I appeased my doctors, counsellors and Nancy by participating in the counselling sessions and took the medication. I soon began to feel better (normal). Soon I cut back on my counselling sessions as I thought I didn't need them anymore and was 'better'. As a result, I didn't stick to the regime of taking my medication. This peak of normalisation as I call it didn't last that long, and I soon began to spiral out of control again.

This intermittent counselling and medication regime continued for the next six years until I hit the wall of reality - in the hardest way possible.

In my typical male way, I felt that admitting to having these conditions was considered non '*macho*'; definitely nothing you talked about in the open. I internalised the problem which only made it worse. If I ever did admit to having these conditions, more often than not I was told to "harden up"or "snap out of it", by further reinforcing my stereotypical beliefs, that only weak-willed people suffer from PTSD. It was definitely the era when you would never tell your employer you suffered from any kind of mental health issue as it would become career-limiting. This long period of suffering in silence and acting as if nothing was wrong and that I was on top of things, only coiled that internal spring to snapping/breaking point, which it did in 2012.

I started to fear authority. Every time I was required to meet with, or report to, any higher authority, I would immediately go into a self-doubting mode. My fear would be that I'd made a mistake in something I'd submitted or done, or even worse, being caught out for non-performance. This was when my self-confidence started to crumble in *everything* I set out to do. The more my self-esteem declined, the better an actor I had to become. This placed tremendous internal pressures on me and I could only store them up for so long.

This is where the actor in me came to the forefront, at the beginning of taking up each of these positions I portrayed someone who was highly professional, outcome driven and career orientated. I could only keep up this front for so long before it all started to fall apart. I knew internally things were starting to spiral and I was turning to other vices as avoidance tools. As each 18-month cycle came around, I grew more and more dependent on my vices, and in particular, alcohol which not only kept me away from my family but also started to have a significant impact on my working life and health.

I told myself,so long as I could change jobs on a regular basis, I would be able to maintain my so-called dignity and professional career. Looking back, I can see that while I was able to play the actor for an extended period of time in each instance the screen started to crack and other people could see behind the scenes. I was subconsciously aware of this but didn't really have the tools to deal with these downward spirals into darkness.

I can look back and wonder now how many middle and senior managers in various positions are experiencing mental health issues and are trying to hide from themselves and others, effectively burning other good employees and teams.

As this cycle started to evolve each one of the rotations became worse than the one before. The avoidance and use of alcohol gradually became catastrophic. I divorced myself from my family and parental duties to the extent where basically when it came to the family, *"I was missing in action"*! These are years I can never get back; years I missed seeing my family grow and my children become teenagers and young adults.

I had basically abandoned Nancy and left her to manage the family unit in every way but physically. But in 2007 I finally left. I had to move to Canberra for a work contract and I was very excited about at the time, but this meant my living away from Nancy and the kids. After coming home every second weekend for a while, I eventually found it much easier to simply stay away and keep hiding out in my solitary bubble.

I should have been there for Nancy and the kids, anticipating the years that we would grow older together watching our family grow and develop. During these years we also missed out on what normal families do, like taking vacations together, experiencing lifes' moments as we all chased dreams that make lasting memories. The only things I have to look back on for this period of time in my life are old photographs and memorabilia that Nancy has kept of the kids. When I look back at these, there is always one common denominator, and that is the 'missing husband and father'.

11

At War With Myself

Did I make the right decisions in Afghanistan? The ongoing personal struggle around ethics and morality is even more present today than it ever was in Afghanistan. My role in Afghanistan involved making many decisions which at the time were based on all the information I had available to me. The pressures of command and my role in the intelligence directorate saw me making decisions daily which also had impacts on how the HQ executed its role and mandate throughout Afghanistan. These decisions were never taken lightly. One of the dichotomies of being a professional intelligence officer, is that very rarely does the public hear about successful operations. It's only when operations don't succeed or involve tragic outcomes such as collateral damage does the spotlight come on and questions are asked about your actions.

I grew up in a family unit based on the norms of the Anglo-Saxon Christian family in the 1970's and 80's in Australia. Throughout my school years, my life centred on being part of the family and learning about the rights and wrongs of the society I lived in. Throughout this period there was an extremely high expectation of behaviour, respect and doing the right thing. For me this was learned within the family unit, schools I went to, and the organisations I belonged to such as scouts, army cadets, and sporting teams.

Socialisation during this period was about involvement with social groups and being accepted within those groups; being part of something, whether it was a sporting team school unit or a close bond with friends. Social belonging has always remained important to me and makes up the fibre that I am and have been to this day. Not knowing it then but on reflection, being part of these groups meant that I was being taught and instilled with a set of values and behaviour. One of those behaviours was that it was not always deemed appropriate for males to show emotion and talk about their feelings. The defunct leadership model around 'the great man theory' reinforces that you never show weakness. These traits of an effective leader are typical masculine traits. This set of particular behaviours is one that has haunted me from an early age, throughout my military career and into my private life. It has had a catastrophic effect on my ability to contain thoughts and feelings which are deemed socially unacceptable to talk about. As for many men of my generation, the expected norm of restraining emotions has had a devastating effect on my family and me.

During my Australian based military training, it was always instilled in us that we were learning the art of war. However, this also involved certain rules and norms that must be obeyed in any conflict. I remember particularly those sessions around discussions of the rules of war and international conventions you must follow as a professional soldier. This training and my family background meant that I had deeply instilled in myself a very high level of ethics and morality around the conduct of conflict. This underlying premise and my professional training ensured that in any decisions that I made, they were not only based on fact or intelligence but had that underlying benchmark-whatever I was doing was morally ethical and purely professional.

What must be understood since time immemorial is throughout conflict there have always been instances when decisions have been made based on the best available information held at the time, however unfortunately sometimes things don't always go to plan, and there may be collateral damage. When talking about collateral damage for me, it means there has been human suffering, not only injury or loss of life but the destruction of people's homes, infrastructure and society in general. Being part of the HQ in Kabul that was tasked with executing the war on terror and eliminating high-value targets meant I was part of that collective group. I was part of the HQ, and sometimes not all operations went as planned. It has taken me many years to realise that any decisions I made while on operations were always part of the collective process and not my decision alone.

Even in the process of writing about this internal struggle, I have within me about being part of a military organisation tasked with conducting operations, raises my anxiety levels. I feel tightness in my chest, shortness of breath, the clenching of my gut muscles and sweaty palms. I find it hard to separate the good and bad thoughts. Even to this day, I struggle with processing news about conflict or human suffering of any nature and making any rational thought about it. What I see and read about human suffering, as a result of conflicts around the world causes my sense of morality and ethics to come strongly into play. This is where my rational brain has trouble separating instances of being in charge of operational decision-making more than a dozen years ago, *vs* just hearing about other situations evolving around the world now, that I personally have no involvement with.

My thoughts around analysing current world events is influenced by a *real* appreciation about visualising what it looks like as opposed to a 'boys own comic strip' about beating the bully which is the narrative for those who don't really understand the reality of war. I think our spectrum of violence is also extended. Live or die scenario's really do require us to use absolute force and fight dirty, to win at all costs. After all, it is exactly that - a life and death situation. But maybe this can be an 'eyes, throat, knees' approach rather than a more graduated response in our society. This is the focus for Close Quarter Battle fighting - fighting dirty to win or get away - eyes to blind or obscure vision, throat to choke or impact on a person's ability to breathe properly, and knees to maim or affect their mobility to move effectively.

To me, this is all about just being a normal human being, who like any other father, husband, brother, or son can be easily placed into a position where demands are made of them in challenging situations.

Whether it's to get up and check on the 'bump' outside in the middle of the night to protect your family or the decision around the 'end of life' for a family pet. My ability post-Afghanistan to separate the 'then' from the 'now' internally is compromised, and I believe it's because of having had to make serious life and death decisions in times of war. Not everyone you meet can understand how that feels because in this day and age it's not a common thing to know anything about.

In the same way as it affects soldiers in a combat zone, CEO's and entrepreneurs must also face the tough demands of decision making that can be incredibly stressful. For example, having to make people redundant when you know it's going to dramatically and negatively affect either an individual, team, family, company, or in some cases an entire town or industry. When it comes to the weight of big decision making sometimes those demands don't actually come fully to your own consciousness at the time. This can be because of your moral fibre, professional training or whatever context of the group you're part of at the time. In my case, those demands that were made on me were reasonable and in the context of my professional role and ability. It wasn't until some years later that I started to question the decisions I've made while on operations. I look back post-Afghanistan, and I see that at times I was placed in a position of responsibility both personally and professionally, to make some hard calls.

In hindsight, *to the best of my knowledge* at that time, I made the *right* calls, but nonetheless, my brain just can't switch off to the fact that every decision I now make has a life-and-death ring to it. Even though the rational part of my brain says, 'I'm at home in New Zealand where I'm safe my family are safe, and the chances of anything catastrophic happening is remote'. For example, riding on a bus or train in Wellington New Zealand, arguably one of the safest places in the world, I am caught up in the stress of being in a confined space where the person who just boarded might be a suicide bomber. My hyper-sensitivity just won't settle down and allow for the difference in location. I still can't go into a restaurant, theatre or plane without having to go through the mental arithmetic of where all the exits are, checking carefully every person who is also present. This is a major part of how my PTSD affects me on a daily basis.

12

The Decline of 2011

Despite 2011 being a great year in terms of my career, it was also the year my life started to completely unravel as the constant pressures of so many internal struggles became harder to cover up and hide from those around me. My inner conflicts and constant monitoring of everything and everyone around me were very much starting to affect me both mentally and physically.

As the Director of the Strategy for the Royal New Zealand Airforce (RNZAF), I had achieved a number of significant goals. The first of these was I had delivered to the RNZAF, a high-level command and control structure that would support the introduction of new capabilities and ensure higher standards of safety and engineering. In this new position, the Chief of the Airforce asked me to coordinate and develop this corporate restructure for formal implementation on the 11 December 2011.

This powerful, high-pressure, and demanding role fitted perfectly within my boundaries and capabilities. It once again forced me into my perceived comfort zone of working within a high-pressure situation and having deadlines to deliver. Most of the time I worked autonomously under the Chief of the Airforce and at times called on small teams of subject-matter experts to provide me with background information and future options.

While this was an exciting and fulfilling time at work, my personal life was once again spiralling out of control. The pressures placed on me were what I expected and thrived upon. I also enjoyed having the confidence of my superiors. However, as mentioned in the past even though I was receiving praise for my efforts, every time I got a call to go and meet with the Chief, I would straight away delve into that subconscious fear about what I must have done incorrectly? It was that self-doubting mode that always came to the surface. This lack of confidence in my own ability was progressively getting worse and was reaching the level where I would doubt my own ability to actually do anything or achieve anything, regardless of how small that might be.

One of the downsides of being tasked with doing any organisational restructure of roles is some individuals may lose their jobs. The knowledge of this also affected me as I personally felt responsible for people's lives, not as a sense of life and death, but their personal and working lives. As much as I tried to rationalise this aspect of the job for me, it was still a 'life and death' scenario I continued to carry with me from Afghanistan. No matter how I personally and professionally tried to justify my decisions and recommendations, I still felt a very personal responsibility towards these impacted individuals.

The other downside of taking on such a task is those people who see their livelihood and professional careers being threatened, at times became quite hostile towards me. Some of this hostility was openly displayed while some of it was more surreptitious. No matter how it was directed at me, I built up an outward composure of resilience and professionalism, while internally I was deeply hurt and at times angry. I did manage to complete the task and meet the deadline, gaining the following high praise for my work. . However, I still questioned my ability and confidence.

"Bill is one of those rare talents that can simplify complex issues to their core, develop strategy, and then lead the implementation of the plan.

Bill worked for me when I was the Chief of the Royal New Zealand Air Force, and he was instrumental in helping clarify our strategy, shaping the set-up of a most efficient Office of Strategy Management, as well as managing a significant piece of reorganisation to a tight deadline and with minimal resources.

It is Bill's dual strengths of intellectual imagination and pragmatic management that I found so invaluable. He is an astute reader of situations and has a sharp sense of social awareness and a well-developed political savvy - this combined with a good sense of humour allows him to shape outcomes as a senior team member most effectively."

Air Vice-Marshal Graham Lintott, RNZAF

In addition to the project I was working on for the RNZAF, I was also a member of a small group of four individuals whom all this held similar positions for the Army, Navy and the NZDF HQ. Our combined task was to formulate a restructuring of the New Zealand Defence Force HQ. While I saw it as privileged to be chosen for such an important project, I would constantly ask myself whether I was good enough to be in this team or whether I had the professional ability and standing to be among these accomplished individuals. Outwardly I once again portrayed as a very confident and professional person. Internally I was starting to get very conflicted as my confidence and self-doubting was really starting to take hold, bubbling away at the back of my brain 24 hours a day. While this was happening, I had to shift up another gear in the acting stakes to show everything was normal and I was on top of the *usual stresses of everyday work life* in such an environment. This is a normal cycle for most people as we all have stresses in our lives with our personal and working lives and occasionally have blips on the radar. This is nothing unusual it just comes with the territory of any working environment.

At the start of 2012 with the previous primary task behind me, I began to grasp for projects which would require a similar high-intensity commitment. During the early months of 2012 with the lack of direction and determination, I began in earnest another 18-month downward spiral. I started spending less and less time at work and making excuses as to why I had to leave early. This once again was about me implementing my avoidance tools and in particular using alcohol.

It got to the stage where I left work under the guise of having to go and do something or meet with somebody. Then I would head straight to my local bar where I would drink all afternoon and most days into the early evening. It was at this stage the family saw very little of me and what they did see was a husband, father coming home drunk just about every night of the week and going straight to bed. Some days I would wake up and ring work and say that I was working from home on a project or I was ill and unable to attend. Throughout this period I would seek solace in the local bar with a group of individuals whom I thought were my friends, but were mere acquaintances, and used them as an excuse to stay drinking.

Those days I did stay at home, I found myself starting to drink on my own. I'd advanced from just having a beer, to drinking wine, cider and spirits; whatever was on the agenda for that day. I would often be in bed asleep when Nancy came home, or in the local bar topping up. One of the godsends, if any, of this period was that our daughter was attending a boarding school, so she was somewhat hidden from this daily routine of mine. Unfortunately, it was Nancy who was again was the one who had to bear the brunt of my behaviour.

By mid-January 2012, I had decided that life was just too difficult and while I was doing a great job of ruining my own life, more importantly, I had ruined the life of my family. At this stage, I was only taking my medication intermittently and receiving minimal counselling. It's important to note here that the decision to not take my medication and limit my counselling sessions was because I knew that I had entered the depths of despair and didn't want to admit to myself that things were as bad as they were. I was fooling myself. As much as Nancy and other close friends tried to talk to me or help me, I refused their advances, because internally I perceived I was in control of myself. When you are in a major depressive episode you become upbeat, you have found a solution – unfortunately others interpret this as 'they are on the mend'. It was with this feeling of control that I made the decision - Nancy and the children would be better off without me in their lives.

On the 9th of February 2012, after seeing Nancy off to work and saying I was going to work from home, I knew it was time to implement my plan. I had thought about ending my life for some weeks, and now all the planets were aligned - today was to be the day! Over the previous couple of days, I'd surreptitiously ensured my personal and financial affairs were in order and my will and other relevant documents were readily available for Nancy. Just after she left for work, I went down to the local supermarket and bought my fill of cider and wine which was going to be my poison for the day. I noticed I was surprisingly calm and felt quite content with what I was about to do.

I spent the morning and early afternoon steadily drinking and listening to my favourite tunes. I also brought out the photographs of the family; Nancy and the children. On reflection now, looking at the photos made me feel content and happy, and I suppose I knew those smiling faces in the photographs would continue even after a brief bout of sorrow after my passing. It made me glad when I knew Nancy and the children would after a period of grief, live their lives again and be content and happy and no longer with that burden of having a troubled husband and father. Fortunately, or unfortunately, depending on whose perspective you look at it, I am still here to today.

Around three thirty in the afternoon I decided it was time to implement the final phase of my plan. I went into the garage where I had assembled a rope over one of the rafters and tied a loop on one end.

Luckily Nancy returned home from work a little after 4pm, and found me in the garage semi-conscious. This was only because the rope I'd used was an old climbing rope which stretched allowing the stool I was standing on to take my weight. My wife cut me down and immediately rang for an ambulance and the mental health crisis action team which also meant she had to ring the police.

I had now become an attempted suicide statistic in New Zealand officially, unfortunately, one of too many. I was admitted to hospital where I stayed for two days.

13

Twice Lucky!

After being under observation and some initial assessments, I was released. The hospital stay in reality only treated my symptoms from my attempted suicide and not the root cause. The resident psychiatrist spoke to me and said I had the option of going home or agreeing to admit myself into the hospital mental institution. After a brief conversation with Nancy, it was agreed that I would commit myself. On entry to the institution my belongings were taken from me including my shoelaces and belt, and I was placed in a room containing a bed. There was nothing in the room for me to read or a TV to watch. I was just put in this room and left to twiddle my thumbs.

The only time I was allowed to exit the room was to go and have a cigarette, and then I had to return to the room. Minutes seemed like hours, hours seemed like days, and I just sat in the room ruminating about what I had just done. By late afternoon on day one in the institution, I received another visit from the resident psychiatrist who explained to Nancy and me what was going to happen next. I was told that I was going to be referred to alcohol and drug counselling.

Ironically, he could not give me an appointment as the counsellors were all booked up. Over worked and under staffed.

We were also told that sometime in the near future I would receive further assessments and they would put a plan in place. This didn't eventuate in time! As I had self-admitted myself to the institution, I decided that afternoon to discharge myself and go home. I made this decision at the behest of Nancy, but I also thought that I had hit rock bottom, had my wake-up call, and now everything could only go up. I also believed that I was not a *mental case* and didn't need to be admitted into an institution. The sooner we got out of there, the sooner I could dismiss the stigma of being mentally unstable.

During the ensuing two weeks, home life remained a struggle while I stayed in complete denial that anything was wrong. I also continued to use my avoidance tools of alcohol and isolation from the family. Looking back over this two week period there is not a lot I can remember, but in hindsight I can see very clearly that I was continuing to decline.

One incident during this period remains extremely vivid and disturbing. During one of my frequent trips to the local bar, I was seated at a table with some acquaintances drinking heavily. It now it had become common knowledge that I had attempted to end my life, as these things are hard to hide in a small local community. One of the individuals sitting at the table commented that I was a failure and that he was going to go down to the local hardware store and buy some rope. He then went on to explain that he was going throw it over the beam and show me how to hang myself properly. Instantly I went into a state of shock and mentally shut down and couldn't say anything. A number of the local veteran community heard this comment and removed him from the bar.

I sat there at the moment for what seemed like an eternity trying to process what had just happened. People around me told me not to worry about it and that he was an idiot and I shouldn't take any notice what he said. It's easy for people to say that. However, it only further convinced me that I was a complete failure - not only with regards to what I had done in my life, but I couldn't even get my suicide attempt right. The damage had already been done!

On the 12 March 2012, I made another attempt to end my life. I had reached the point where I believed that everything I'd done in my life had been a failure and there was nothing else I could do but to rid my family of the burden of me. Everything seemed to be closing in around me; my bubble had become impenetrable. Even though there was turmoil in my thoughts, there was also a great sense of calm in knowing that all of this pain was going to end soon.

I once again saw Nancy off to work and told her not to worry. This was my last time I believed I would see her. Subsequently, I have talked with her, and we discussed this event in great detail. I'm overlooking the fact that the psychological pressure on her was immense and it's so important for anyone going through supporting their loved one in crisis to consider this. She has written her version of events and perspective at the end of this book. We often forget about the other person in the relationship and what they are going through! She was torn on whether she could trust me to be on my own or whether she just had to continue working and hope events wouldn't repeat them self. Nancy couldn't afford to be my carer 24/7, she still had to work, and I also insisted I could be trusted and had already stood on that cliff looking over the precipice into the abyss.

I had once again formulated a plan to take my life and it involved taking a drug overdose. I searched the house high and low for all my prescription medication including all those I had not taken over the years. Looking back subconsciously, I asked the question why had I kept my unused drugs for years. I was able to lay my hands on hundreds of different types of prescription medication including those for depression, anxiety, blood pressure and pain. Once again I started the day out drinking heavily and going through that routine of looking at photographs, playing my favourite music and taking medication to send me into that sense of calmness and that everything was going to be okay shortly. By about three o'clock that afternoon after continually drinking and regularly taking more and more prescription medication, I slipped into that feeling of contentment and calmness and then drifted off.

Nancy happened to return home from work early, and as she entered the house, found me on the kitchen floor, floating in and out of consciousness and convulsing. Nancy instantly called the ambulance and police and got our next door neighbour who was a fireman and paramedic. They administered first aid and tried to do what they could until emergency services arrived. I know the emergency responders had trouble stabilising me before they could transport me to the emergency department. The ambulance also stopped en-route as I needed further stabilisation as I began to drift away again. Once I was stabilised in the emergency department, I spent a period in ICU until they believed I was out of any danger. After transferring me to a ward, I started to gain some form of consciousness. I was not out of the danger zone yet.

The first recollection I have in the hospital was when I woke up, and I saw my wife and my daughter sitting beside my bed. I believe it was in that instant that something clicked in my mind, saying this is where it all stops now! It has been from that moment I made a commitment to myself that I was going to overcome this illness. While in the hospital I was told by the specialists that if it wasn't for Nancy arriving home early from work and with the help of the fireman from next door, I would most likely not have made it. They also told me that the amount of prescription medication I had taken may have damaged my liver and kidneys and it would be a wait and see situation to see if they were going to recover. Also during the initial period in the hospital, the overdose affected my overall body muscle control. I was unable to walk or support myself, and I couldn't even hold a glass of water. This would only get better over time, and now I have full muscular control, and my internal organs have recovered to be within the normal range of function.

I am one bloody lucky person!

Following my release from hospital I was contacted by the RNZAF who informed me that my current contract with them was going to be terminated early as a result of my medical condition. In February 2012 I still had some months to run on my contract. I was also informed that it would be in my interests and that of my fellow work colleagues if I come in over the weekend to clear my desk and gather my personal belongings. I found this extremely troubling especially after what I've just been through and my then current state of mind.

Nancy and I were shocked to hear that this is how I was being treated. Apart from being upsetting, this outraged me and made me even more confused. These actions taken by the RNZAF HR department was very troubling and represented a complete lack of understanding of my situation and of how to deal with somebody who had PTSD and had just attempted suicide.

It epitomises the thought process back then. The organisation didn't understand how to address the situation and thought by sweeping it under the carpet the problem would just go away. Their reluctance to face up to the situation was deeply disturbing and represented the attitude back then that it was easier not to face up to the situation but to keep it hidden.

I discussed as best I could the situation with Nancy and in my anger, stubbornness, and personal pride, I decided I wouldn't succumb to their request to clear my desk over the weekend period but instead go to work on the Friday lunchtime to do it. To my astonishment people at work had heard about my situation, however as was done back then and now, nobody talked about it openly as they found it uncomfortable and confronting. Even so, the reception I got from most of my colleagues when I did turn up to work was nothing but understanding and supportive. Of course, there were those individuals who found it hard to interact with me or even talk to me as the situation was too confronting and uncomfortable for them to deal with. Those colleagues who did offer their support and understanding are still to this day supportive. We keep in contact, and they are genuinely interested in my recovery.

When my NZDF Medical Officer was made aware of the situation, he was astounded and approached the then Deputy Chief of the Air Force to let him know that this was an appalling way to treat somebody who had suffered such an injury. If it hadn't been for the Medical Officer's intervention, I would have been discharged early and become just another statistic, not to be talked about!

On the 8 of March 2012, I was called to a meeting with the RNZAF and then told my contract would cease effective from of 16th of April 2012. "I was told that I was not to report for duty during the period 8th March to 16th April as this was a period of 'duty of care' to allow for my circumstances." To me at the time this meant out of site out of mind. PTSD and suicide was, and still is, very much a taboo subject.

On reflection about this particular incident, even now five years later it upsets me greatly, but I also recognise it as a reflection of the wider attitudes of society and the military. Then and now, we fail to discuss anything about mental health and the issues associated with it. We still live behind the facade where being 'bullet-proof' is a seen as part of the leadership model.

├───────┤

Since these events in 2012, I have always thought about those emergency service personnel, police and hospital staff; what they had to go through and see as a result of my actions. I know I'm only one of very many individuals with whom they have to deal with as a result of suicide attempts. I acknowledge that if it weren't for these brave and selfless people, I wouldn't be here today to tell my story. I know it is their professional duty to help all individuals in distress. However, there must be a toll on them personally by having to deal with such situations as mine. Often it is these people who are overlooked for recognition for *just doing their job*. I know from my group PTSD treatment in Sydney that some of these very selfless people can also be sufferers of PTSD. In my eyes, it is they who are real heroes in society.

I know I probably can't thank these people individually but hope through my story they get the recognition they deserve.

14

The After Marth

My First AA Meeting

My stomach was in knots, my anxiety through the roof, the tremors almost uncontrollable, and I was bathed in sweat. However, I knew in the back of my mind that I had to take this significant step if I was going to embark on a journey of recovery. I remember standing outside one of the local community halls where Alcoholics Anonymous (AA) held its meetings. Standing on the footpath outside I was consumed with trepidation as to whether I would walk through those doors and finally admit that to get my life back on track, I would have to deal with my issues one step at a time.

I knew that for the past eight years I had used alcohol as one of my PTSD avoidance tools . When I finally plucked up the courage to enter the hall and take my first major step toward recovery and admit that the use of alcohol was my most preferred avoidance tool. I was surprised to see some familiar faces whom I had no idea had issues with alcohol – it is truly anonymous. I was warmly greeted by all those who were present, and I instantly realised that this was the first major step towards the recovery. Even though the individuals at the meeting made me feel welcome the anxiety and fear were still very much present. I remembered making myself a cup of coffee and was unable to drink it because my tremors were so bad I couldn't hold the cup without spilling the coffee all over myself. This only added to the anxiety of my first meeting at AA. I had mixed emotions during the first session,I was openly showing a significant weakness in my character, and on the other hand, a little bit of pride in that I'd admitted there was an issue and I had started to deal with. This mix of emotions still continues to this day. However, I have learned through my residential PTSD program that I shouldn't concentrate so much on the negative feelings but reward myself for the positive steps I've taken.

Leaving Hospital

After being discharged from hospital for the second time on the 19 March 2012, I knew I'd reached the depths of those dark places and there was only one way to go and that was up. It was then I knew I had to take control of my life and destiny. While attending AA was the first major step in my recovery I started to implement other initiatives to aid my recovery. These involved weekly, and sometimes twice weekly, sessions with my clinical psychologist and also finally attending an alcohol and drug rehabilitation program. In addition to trying to aid my mental recovery I also had to start looking after my health, and as such, I implemented a strict physical rehabilitation program. At my gym, I was lucky enough to have a personal trainer with whom I could confide and openly talk about my issues which helped her develop a fitness program for me that was gradual and attainable.

The first couple months of my recovery seemed to be on track. However, it soon became apparent that the expectations I'd set myself for the time frame of my recovery were too high. As I charged headlong into my recovery phase, it soon became apparent that my issues weren't going to be solved overnight. This, however, proved to be a double-edged sword as my ambitions soon outstripped my progress. This led to a severe bout of depression, amid despair that I was never going to overcome my mental health issues. Adding to this was also the realisation that I would never be that old Bill of the past - high achiever, confident and always striving for perfection.

Adding to my severe depressive episodes was the expectations of the majority of people around me asking when was I going to be better and when was I was going to return to work? This additional pressure was immense and added to my internal confusion and self-doubt because, on the one hand, I knew that my mental state was far more severe than I knew, while at the same time I thought I had to snap out of this and put it behind me and just get back to work. This contrary confusion is debilitating and continually revisits me to this day.

I quickly found out that there was a real ignorance, especially around PTSD in veterans and in general. It soon became apparent by *admitting* I have PTSD, there was a reluctance within the military and the general community to accept this condition as being one that is actually severely debilitating and permanent. People saw the injury of PTSD as no different to any physical injury. In that, if you break a leg you know that in six to eight weeks time the bone would be healed and the physical injury was gone. As time went on, I was consistently asked why my recovery has taken so long and when will I be healed?

15

Agencies and Confusion

The Timeline

March, July & September 2006 - Psychiatrist Assessments for VANZ

16 January 2007 - Psychiatrist Assessments for VANZ

9 February 2012 - Hanging attempt

14March 2012 - Overdose attempt

1st May 2012 - Assessment with Physiatrist for VANZ – 3 hours

18 May 2012 - Assessment with Physiatrist for ACC – 2 hours

23 Apr 2013 - Assessment with Physiatrist for VANZ reassessment of a temporary condition which was to expire 20 May 2013, pending a decision as to whether my condition was permanent! Recommendation it was permanent – 2 hours

After leaving the NZDF, I was put under the care of New Zealand's Veterans Affairs Department. As my condition had been accepted as a war injury, they took on my case and have been managing it for me ever since. Under their legislation and guidelines, they are constrained as to what medical interventions are available to veterans. In my case, any medical treatment available to me under Veterans Affairs is counselling and medication. However, they have been able to help with my recovery by providing access to physical rehabilitation programs. I would like to note that my Veterans Affairs case managers have been excellent and sympathetic to my needs. The issue which underlies the ability of Veterans Affairs to provide assistance is it is always a lengthy and stressful application process. The medical interventions for veterans with PTSD are insufficient in New Zealand compared to those available in Australia, United Kingdom, Canada and the United States. There is no recognition of alternative forms of treatment both medically and psychologically which are available to our Allied veterans.

Case Managers at Veterans Affairs are the frontline individuals who deal with all the issues and problems of the veterans. These case managers work tirelessly and are dedicated to trying to get the best help that is available for their clients. The key issue that arises here is these case managers are hamstrung by the legislation and guidelines they operate under, causing lengthy delays and in some cases critical delays in getting help to a veteran. The other issue that impedes the decision-making process about getting help to veterans, is the slow processing time reliant on second and third line decision-makers who see to have little empathy for the veterans' needs. They are so bogged down with following the lengthy bureaucratic legislation and in particular determining whether the veteran has met the required medical threshold, for an application to be approved.

In my particular case, I had been assessed in 2006 and diagnosed with PTSD but I had to attend further evaluations with the same Psychiatrist in July, and September 2006, and yet again in January 2007.

On the 1st of May 2012 after my two suicide attempts, I was once again sent to the same consulting psychiatrist for a re-evaluation of my condition. This was a harrowing three-hour interview within which I had to relive my experiences once again. I can see the need for such a reassessment. However, the length of the interview is determined by the requirements of Veterans

Affairs to follow a long and convoluted assessment process.

During the same period, I was placed on workers compensation which is administered by the New Zealand Government Insurer. From 2012 to 2015 I was administered under the scheme by an agreement between the government Insurer and the NZDF. My case manager during this period was exceptional and understood my needs and tried to make it as least stressful as possible. However, he was also restricted in what assistance he could provide as he had to work under strict guidelines, which made the process difficult to manoeuvre through.

As my worker's compensation claim was being administered by a different agency, there was another requirement for me to meet with the same psychiatrist on the 18 May 2012 only seventeen days after my first assessment. This was again daunting and confusing. However, the Psychiatrist explained to me that we had to go through this three-hour interview process yet again because he had different guidelines and reporting requirements for the government insurer. After the turmoil of the previous five months, my mental state was extremely fragile, and the claim process was entirely unsympathetic, as I was forced to relive my trauma multiple times for two different organisations, just to satisfy their respective archaic and bureaucratic assessment guidelines.

On the 23 Apr 2013 I attended yet another full-blown assessment for VANZ to obtain a new report on my disability.

"We need to know Mr Blaikie's present level of disability and if it is permanent or temporary".

As my temporary condition was to expire on the 20 May 2013 pending a decision as to whether my condition was permanent! The assessment recommended that my condition was at the *"permanent"* level of disability because of my vulnerability to relapse would continue.

This not only placed enormous stress and anxiety on me but that stress and anxiety also flowed through to my family. At no point during this period was Nancy or our children given any opportunity to receive counselling or support for dealing with their stress and anxiety as a result of my condition. Nancy is not entitled to any support from Veterans Affairs as it is not *her* injury!

It has been widely recognised around the world that the family of PTSD sufferers also suffer what is known as secondary PTSD, in that families have to live with the trauma of the veteran and all their issues.

Since 2012 I am required to obtain a doctor's certificate every three months indicating I am [still] not fit to return to full-time employment. Being stuck in this gridlocked process, I feel that I have to justify my injury/illness every three months (to this day) if I want to continue to receive workers compensation. Having to adhere to this process constantly reminds me of how much I am struggling with PTSD.

In addition to these three*monthly justification requirements, the insurer's aim is to get you off their books as soon as possible and back into the workplace. One of those indignant methods is by sending you for occupational assessments with various recruitment agencies and medical professionals. Over the years, this is placed an immense amount of stress and anxiety on me which was again transferred to my family, each time I have to attend one of the assessments. One of these evaluations required me to attend three different sessions to ascertain what skills I had and at what levels and what possible avenues of employment I should pursue. These assessments were based on an individual who may have had physical injury or impairment and then look at what type of alternative employment would be most suitable. These evaluations did not take into account mental injury and my ability to process what it was that I wanted, let alone was capable of, after a lifelong career in the military.

On one occasion I was referred to a medical, occupational physician. I remember this particular appointment, as it proved to be one of the most stressful situations I had been placed in since 2012. I knew it was going to be difficult so I asked Nancy to attend the appointment with me. From the outset, I knew it was not going to end well as the doctor seemed to be oblivious to my mental state and how PTSD affects an individual. He was clinical in the way he went about his assessment in that asked me to identify all the skills that I had obtained during my working life. After this, he then went on to look at all the positions I held throughout my career and decided that there was no practical reason why I could not continue to be employed in any position equivalent to what I held in 2012 including any high-level management positions. The report to the insurer indicated that he saw no reason why I could not be employed in the same or similar roles I'd held before 2012. Again, this is one of those processes the insurer puts you through to get you off their books as soon as possible. During this assessment, my anxiety levels were such that my tremors were almost uncontrollable and at various times during the evaluation, I broke down and sobbed. The doctor showed little empathy throughout the evaluation, and at times Nancy had to intervene to comfort and reassure me.

These processes may well be a necessary evil, but the one glove fits all approach does not work with those who have a mental injury. Over the past five years, this constant pressure and hounding from the insurer to justify my illness and my inability to return to full-time work not only adds to the anxiety, stress and depression but is a constant reminder that I have PTSD. I feel that I am constantly not only battling my own demons as result of PTSD but fighting the insurer and the process of which I'm stuck and see no end to.

Constantly having to deal with two agencies and two case managers both of whom have to operate within two different legislations and guidelines is stressful. Over the years trying to deal with this imposed regime, it has led to several breakdowns, and at times these have been severe. Not only was there significant depressive episodes, but I constantly feel my integrity is under attack. Thus my self-confidence suffers as a consequence. This cycle seems like it will never end and I feel I'll never be able to let go of my PTSD because I am always under attack.

This constant feeling of being under attack means I revert to my defence mechanism that everything around me has a "life-and-death" consequence. Living with this sense of hypervigilance day in, day out, takes its toll emotionally and physically. No matter how much exercise and sleep I get, I always have that feeling of being exhausted. The emotional toll is a daily occurrence because I haven't been able to go one day without thinking about PTSD, my illness and the challenges thrown up every day. It is important to note here that Nancy and I also have to deal with those normal stresses in everybody's life around family, finances and just day-to-day things life throws at us.

———

In April 2016 my worker's compensation claim was transferred from the NZDF to the Government insurer (in New Zealand this is Accident Compensation Commission, ACC), and I received a new case manager. It wasn't until May 2016 after much lobbying on my behalf and Nancy's active intervention that we were finally able to have a *joint* meeting with my case managers from Veteran's Affairs and ACC, to discuss a way forward on my treatment and rehabilitation. This initial meeting took place at the insurer's offices as their case manager was not permitted to meet off-site in a neutral venue. This already raised my anxiety levels knowing that in my mind I was putting myself into a hostile situation, in a place where I had no control. No matter how many times I told myself that we were just meeting in an office block in New Zealand my mind kept telling me that I was entering into a hostile situation similar to what I found myself in 2004, when I met the warlord in Herat.

Nancy and I were fortunate to have an outstanding advocate attend this meeting with us who had previous experience in dealing with the insurer. During the ensuing days before the meeting, I prepared an open statement for myself to read. It was incredibly hard to write my thoughts down to explain my position and what I hoped to achieve from this meeting.

Our advocate opened by asking what experience the ACC case manager had with dealing with veterans suffering from PTSD and also what was her depth of knowledge and expertise with PTSD sufferers. To our astonishment, the case manager admitted that they had little to no experience or knowledge around veterans with PTSD. She did, however, acknowledge their lack of expertise in this area and would take it upon themselves to gain understanding/education about veterans suffering from PTSD and the implications it has for them. (Of note here - at our next *meeting she admitted that she hadn't been able to gain any more knowledge or education around PTSD due to her workload.*)

The meeting progressed with the aim of trying to identify which agency (ACC or VANZ) would provide *what* services and assistance, and *who* would pay for such treatment. With a lot of toing and froing between all participants and my anxiety and stress levels went through the roof. On two occasions I broke down, resulting in my having to leave the room in tears. It was agreed at the conclusion of the meeting that both organisations would work closely together and look at their respective legislations and guidelines to see which agency was responsible for which part of my treatment, rehabilitation and compensation and come up with a plan for managing my case in the future. To this day this is still a matter of contention as there has been no resolution moving forward on how to handle mine or other similar situations. I still to this day have to deal with two case managers, and have two rehabilitation plans from different agencies seeking different outcomes.

I've subsequently been told that this was the first time such a meeting had taken place between the two organisations case managers to deal with an individual's claim/case!

16

The Struggles We Face
Moving Forward

Taking Back Control

After coming out of the hospital in 2012, I took it upon myself to find out more about PTSD - its causes and the effects it has on a human being. My mission was to research PTSD and find as much information as I could about where I could go for help and with whom I could talk to. Probably, the most important issue for me at this time was to try and find a network of individuals who were suffering the same injury so that we could share experiences and learn from each other. To my amazement, there was very little information readily available in New Zealand about veterans with PTSD and how to cope with it. What I did find is there was a myriad of information on the Internet available through veteran's services amongst our allied nations. Back in 2012, the information available on the Internet was often presented in a clinical form which I found difficult to understand and comprehend. All I was seeking back then was somewhere I could go to understand PTSD in layman's terms which didn't stigmatise it as an injury or illness that one didn't talk about.

The research I conducted confirmed in my mind, that PTSD and mental injuries amongst veterans were more or less taboo subjects. It was something that veterans were not encouraged to talk about or admit to as it was seen as a major character weakness. One of the significant barriers I came across was by admitting I had been diagnosed with PTSD and major depressive disorder, my career within the military was over.

Hence once my contract with the NZDF was over, I had nothing to lose by talking openly about my mental injuries publicly. So, using my skills as an intelligence analyst, I established a website where I could talk about my injury openly and place information about PTSD, and mental injuries within veterans which made it easy to understand and de-stigmatise the condition. While the website was initially for my own understanding, it soon took on a life of its own, and I had numerous people contact me asking for more information or where they could go to seek help. It was then I realised this issue was bigger than me and my own comprehension and it needed to be talked about openly and publicly.

In late 2012 early 2013, I had been contacted by some journalists in New Zealand in both the print and TV media.

On February 4, 2013, a new current affairs show was launched in New Zealand called Seven Sharp. On this first episode, Nancy and I went public with my injury and the effects of PTSD and the consequences it has had for our family. As a result of coming out publicly and talking about these issues, it galvanised public discussion about mental injuries facing modern-day war veterans here in New Zealand. While this issue was not new, it brought to the fore that mental injuries as a result of conflict were here to stay and it was about time we started to take it seriously and de-stigmatise it as a taboo subject. Since the airing of this program and other work done by prominent New Zealand personalities, mental health issues across society have gained a powerful public voice.

One of the very positive outcomes for myself in coming out and talking about my injury is that I have been asked numerous time to speak to NZDF service personnel in various forums about the realities of PTSD and the effects it has on an individual and their family. I have done this by speaking openly about *my* story and *my* journey since I served in Afghanistan in 2004. Nancy and I have also spoken on a number of occasions to community organisations about what the effects of my mental injury have had on us as a family. I continue to speak publicly about this issue as I am passionate that it is acceptable for society to be able to talk about PTSD and mental injuries, especially amongst veterans and their families.

17

Asking for Help

Over the years in my quest to know as much as I could about PTSD and treatment options, I have had to look abroad to see what other countries have on offer for their veterans who are suffering PTSD. To my astonishment, our allied nations not only provide the necessary clinical treatment options which are available here in New Zealand, but they also provide respite care, group therapy and organise communities where like-minded individuals suffering from PTSD and other mental issues are able to go and where veterans can feel supported in a safe environment.

One of the areas I looked into was around group therapy. I look closely at the Australian Department Veterans Affairs (DVA) and what they provide for their veterans. DVA funds numerous private and public hospitals throughout Australia with evidenced-based trauma recovery programs. These programs and guidelines were developed by Phoenix Australia (Centre for Post Traumatic Mental Health), and all hospitals are required to meet DVA National Accreditation Standards for Trauma Recovery Programs. These programs range from both outpatient and inpatient group programs across Australia. There are currently seventeen hospitals across Australia that offer these group programs.[8]

---

[8]   Australian Government Department of Veterans Affairs 2017, http://at-ease. dva.gov.au/professionals/assess-and-treat/ptsd/

18

Trauma Recovery Programs

In early 2015 I approached VANZ to ascertain whether or not there were any such group programs available for veterans in New Zealand. I was informed by VANZ that there were no such programs available in New Zealand and that the only recognised clinical therapies available to veterans were that of Eye Movement Desensitization and Reprocessing (EMDR), and trauma-focused Cognitive-Behavioural Therapy (CBT) and medication. On 22 May 2015, I formally applied to VANZ for assistance and funding to attend a group residential program at the St John of God Hospital, North Richmond, Sydney, Australia. The following is the response I received from VANZ. "Group therapy is not an accepted means of treating PTSD in New Zealand."[9]

After having received this letter from VANZ, I asked for the real reason that I was denied funding and I received this reply of the then VANZ Chief Medical Officer on the 14 July 2015

"As to treatment/ therapy in Australia. VA cannot commit to treatment overseas. If one veteran is provided with international

---

9   VANZ Letter dated 04 June 2015

therapy, then this would lead to many others wanting various treatments which is unaffordable for NZ govt." [10]

Nancy and I were gob smacked at this response, but at least it was the real honest answer. However when we see so much money wasted on non-essential government projects and all the veteran community is asking for is that global best practice for treatment of mental injuries be made available to our veterans. When it comes to physical injuries for veterans, every effort is made to follow the global best practice surgical and rehabilitation solutions developed by our allies in the treatment of wounded service personnel.

Following this refusal to fund treatment by VANZ, I then wrote to the New Zealand Minister of Veterans Affairs, the Hon. Craig Foss, requesting his consideration regarding funding for treatment in the Australian PTSD Program. To our astonishment, we received a letter back from his Private Secretary declining our request. The Minister didn't even have the decency to respond to me directly, as he does not receive submissions from individuals on such matters.

After exhausting all official channels, in trying to get funding to attend the Australian PTSD program, I was left feeling despondent and deeply let down by the government I had served. What made it more frustrating and depressing was I was informed of an ex-NZDF Lieutenant-Colonel who was residing in Australia permanently and who had been diagnosed with PTSD as result of his service in Vietnam and his PTSD had been accepted as a definite condition by VANZ. As he then lived in Australia, and under the reciprocal agreement between our two countries, when dealing with veterans affairs, he was able to access inpatient group PTSD therapy at the Austin Hospital, Melbourne, Victoria.

---

[10]   Email 14/07/15 from NZDF

What is telling about this is that the VANS had informed us that this was not a recognised treatment and yet a veteran under VANZ was able to access PTSD group therapy because he resided in Australia!

At this stage, I'd approached the Australian Department of Veterans Affairs and asked if there was any possibility I could be funded through them to attend a residential PTSD residential group therapy program in Australia, as I previously served fifteen years in the Australian Defence Force (ADF). I was informed by them that as my condition was related to service in the NZDF, I was not entitled to anything under the DVA act. However, I was further informed that if I chose to move back to Australia, I would be eligible for a DVA white card and as such, all available medical treatment options would be open to me including PTSD group therapy.

After exhausting all of my official and bureaucratic options with the New Zealand government in trying to get funding to attend the recognised Australian PTSD group therapy, Nancy and I were left with no choice but to seek crowd funding in New Zealand. We were fortunate enough to meet four exceptional individuals who went out of their way to set up a Crowd Funding Page on the Internet to raise the necessary funds to attend the ten month residential and outpatient PTSD program in Sydney. As part of this fundraising effort, we once again went public to the media, outlining the inadequacies of the current treatment options for veterans here in New Zealand. As a result of speaking publicly to highlight my own personal battles and that of the wider veteran's community, we were fortunate enough to obtain the necessary funds within three weeks.

In September 2016 Nancy, myself and our daughter embarked on this ten month journey of PTSD group therapy. The importance we placed on trying this treatment was that it had proven results, verified by Phoenix Australia, that intensive, prolonged trauma therapy has positive effects. "Prolonged exposure therapy is a gold standard evidenced based treatment for PTSD."[11] The program we attended was run by the St John of God Hospital, North Richmond, Sydney, Australia.

[11] 2017, www.phoenixaustralia.org/expertise/research/current-treatment-trials/restore/

19

The Australian Residential PTSD Program

When we arrived at the hospital for the start of our residential group PTSD program, there was a great feeling of apprehension on my part. For all three of us, going into the unknown for me especially, it seemed that I was going to a dangerous place where I had no idea or control about the outcome. As we entered the hospital grounds, my anxiety levels were shooting through the roof as I knew for the next month at least, I believed I would be in a place where I had little control of my destiny. I was terrified!

The hospital was situated in North Richmond in Sydney, Australia and sits at the base of the Blue Mountains on the outskirts of Sydney. When one enters the hospital grounds, you can't but help to embrace the beauty and serenity of the environment. However, this did little to quell my initial reaction.

Meeting our fellow course members and their families was nerve-racking for all of us, and we were extremely guarded as we were going into the unknown. Meeting the therapists for the first time started to put my mind at ease. I spoke about the goals and aspirations that the course may hold for me. They explained what they hoped we would all achieve. This started by learning to know through this course of therapy, we could see an increase in power or authority over our own intrusive memories. The aim of this was to delve into those traumas which affected us to better manage intrusive memories and hopefully limit the frequency of these intrusive thoughts and nightmares. In doing so, we had to pick two traumatic events that have affected us the most and explore them in depth. This part of the therapy was done through prolonged exposure therapy exploring the trauma and detail. While this process gave me a better understanding about the incidents that caused the injuries,it also helped me understand it's unrealistic to expect all intrusive thoughts could disappear forever.

After going through this process, we were given tools on how to cope with minimising the effects of these intrusive memories which cause a constant hyper-aroused state. The purpose of this was to explore healthy strategies to deal with these emotions, even when the symptoms are intense and inescapable. One of the greatest things I wanted to achieve out of this was to control my self-destructive pattern of behaviour, and emotions which would help lead me to increased self-care and willingness to take control of myself, emotionally, physically and spiritually. As a result of this process, there was growth and self-respect, and I finally started to recognise that I am not a bad person but just an individual who has suffered the mental consequences of war.

One of the primary outcomes *the family* and I wanted to achieve was the development of safe relationships, where I could form more healthy connections and "show a willingness to negotiate, compromise and respect within the family unit." [12]

The first things we did on the course was to write down and visually display those goals each of us wanted to achieve as a result of this program. My visual reminder was a picture of the world map with my thoughts surrounding it. The five goals identified were that:

------

[12]   Harvey 1995 and SJOG Hospital Information Pack 2016

I wanted to emotionally lose weight of all the bad stuff without feeling deprived of the good memories.

I wanted to be able to enjoy life every day.

I again wanted to provide emotional and financial security for my family.

I simply want to love again.

To recognise that the world is still my oyster.

Throughout the course of the therapy over 12 months I was always cognitive of the fact that these were my aspirations and not everything was going to be fixed when I walked out at the end of the program. This program was just another step in understanding what happened to me and how I could better cope with life with the cards that I've been dealt.

Apart from the exposure therapy, we spend a lot of time discussing and understanding the causes of PTSD and how it affects an individual. I found this part of the course/program extremely helpful, especially understanding the structural and functional brain changes that happen when a person suffers a mental injury such as PTSD. It has been extensively researched and proven that sufferers of PTSD demonstrate significant neurological changes in the brain and how it deals with hyperactivity related to trauma. It shows that those people with PTSD have exaggerated startle response and flashbacks, also known as the fight and flight response.[13]

Over the period of the one-month residential element of the program, the group became extremely close and tightly knitted. We lost all our inhibitions and were able to open up emotionally which enabled us to form a strong bond, resulting in complete trust in one another. This was imperative for us if we were going to get the most out of the course. When you open up your heart with all its raw emotions and flaws, you are extremely vulnerable,

---

[13] Psychopharmacology Unit, University of Bristol, Bristol, United Kingdom. david.j.nutt@bristol.ac.uk, https://www.ncbi.nlm.nih.gov/pubmed/14728092

and only then you can start to understand your trauma and how to deal with it as best you can.

The monthly follow-ups sessions for the residential program proved to be invaluable. It allowed me to check in and discuss how I had been travelling in the previous month. It soon became apparent that this program was not a quick fix but a long journey through emotions and learning how to cope with the dramatic ups and downs which is the roller coaster of PTSD. Personally, I found that there was a honeymoon period in the first three months in which I thought that this program might have been my panacea. However, after three months, I came crashing back down to reality with a very dramatic dip in my emotional and physical well-being. This was a reality check! We were told that this roller coaster ride is common among all individuals who undertake prolonged exposure therapy and is nothing to be overly concerned about but just understand that this is all just part of that journey. The following months the spikes and lows in my emotions and behaviour started to occur less often but were still significant.

The inclusion of the family in the program was a real highlight for Nancy and me. It enabled Nancy and the children to understand what I was going through and why. More importantly for me, it provided them with a forum where they could to talk openly about the impact my PTSD had had on their lives. They were able to express themselves without the fear of judgement and any negative reaction from me. This for me was really the first time I heard and understood, and *acknowledged* their pain and suffering and deprivation of a normal life as a result of my injury. Throughout this whole process, I don't think I'd ever shown such raw emotion throughout my lifetime. I learned it's okay to let your emotions *flow* and it is not a weakness to openly show the *full* range of emotions. One of the things that sticks in my mind is after the month long residential phase I felt I was in a safe environment for the very first time since leaving Afghanistan. Every time I returned to the hospital I had an overwhelming feeling of invulnerability and security. I still consider the hospital is my safe zone and hope that someday my own home will feel the same.

The journey through PTSD continues and will be with the family and me forever, however, in the years to come we will hopefully learn to cope with PTSD as being part of our lives but not controlling our existence. During the course of the entire program, I kept a daily diary which enables me to revisit things covered during the program and I continue to learn from it and maybe one day I may be brave enough to publish it as part of my journey so others can learn from it.

20

The Stress of Secrets

Between 1988 and 2012 I had continuously been involved as an intelligence and security professional in many and varied roles. These included the areas of analysis, counter-intelligence, electronic warfare and signals intelligence, intelligence instructor and command of intelligence units at the National and International level.

As an Intelligence professional, I have been required to obtain and maintain the *highest* of national security clearances. To get a top secret security clearance is an incredibly intrusive process but one which is essential to retain the integrity of the individual and also the organisation he or she may work for. It requires the person to bare all about their personal life, both past and present. While I found this intrusive, it was my choice as I elected to be a career intelligence officer. As my chosen career extended over two decades, I was required to undergo numerous security reviews to maintain my security clearance at the highest level.

The stresses that are placed on individuals who works in such highly classified areas, is rarely talked about. The requirement to work in such a secretive and restricted environment, where all information is retained on a need-to-know basis is extremely demanding and stressful. You have to be on your guard 24/7 to ensure that you maintain awareness of what you can and can't talk about. In most ordinary everyday jobs people like to talk about how the day went at work with the family, partner and friends. This is usually part of the general conversation on a day-to-day basis. However, working as an Intelligence professional you are unable to come home and talk about your day and how it went, except in very general terms. So from the outset when I started as an intelligence officer I had to develop the skill of compartmentalising my brain and what I could and couldn't talk about with my wife, children, or any of my friends. The only time that you could talk about your work and what you do was limited to conversations with those people you knew who held a similar security clearance and the requirement 'need to know'. So over a period of two decades, I had to store away all those things I had done in my intelligence career in my own personal vault in my head.

I believe that I developed two personalities: one at work and one outside of work. At first, it was easy to keep the two separate and function relatively normally (What is normal?). However, more recently and in particular after Afghanistan and the cumulative stress that had been building over the last two decades it had become increasingly difficult to separate the two personalities, and unfortunately the work one took over from the non-work one, and everything became a life and death scenario. Some of the tasks that I performed during my career challenged my own personal and professional ethics and morals. As mentioned previously, at times I have struggled with decisions I made which bordered on the fringes of my ethics and morals. A crossover between what I thought was right and wrong have sometimes been a very fine line, and at times I've had to draw a line in the sand and not cross it. The greatest challenge that I faced was making decisions and recommendations in combat operations where there was a risk of casualties; both military and civilian. One of the things that has haunted me particularly from my time in Afghanistan is whether all those decisions and recommendations I made were sound and based on the best information available. In the intelligence world, nothing is 100% certain, and everything is managed by risk. I know that some of those decisions may have resulted in operations not going according to plan and led to casualties. Over the years since Afghanistan, I have struggled with personal guilt over recommendations and decisions that I made during operations. This guilt is real and continually revisits me almost daily. I have questioned everything thousands of times, and yet even by applying sound logic, and knowing that I made the best decisions with the best information available and the best of intentions; I still feel the immense emotion of guilt.

I look back over my career as an intelligence officer, and the overwhelming thought that I have is about those recommendations and decisions that I made. Did they border on my personal ethics and morals to my standards/scale, or did they go over the line?

It is hard to write about this part of my professional career as some people may question my behaviour and conduct as a professional intelligence officer and pass moral judgement on my character. Intelligence has never been an exact science and never will it be, history has proven this over and over again. The dark art of intelligence is a necessary component of government to ensure that we stay one step ahead of the adversary to maintain the safest environment for us to live in.

Over the decades and the various intelligence roles that I've held, I seem only to remember those periods where I struggled ethically and morally and wonder whether or not I've made the *right* decisions. Conversely, I find it hard to recall all of the good and right things I've done in my intelligence career which by far should outweigh any doubts that I have. However by the very nature of the roles that I carried out, there was no place that I could go to discuss my thoughts and concerns. The constant struggle to make the right recommendations and decisions and requirement to keep everything secret and locked away in my mind's vault has had an accumulating effect on my ability to make decisions and more importantly separate out those decisions which are critical and routine. As such, as I previously mentioned, every decision I make reverts back to a life-and-death situation.

Nancy and my friends have to always remind me that not everything is life-and-death and it's okay to make a mistake or get something wrong. That is why in the period leading up to my suicide attempts in 2012 I increasingly turned to alcohol to mask my emotions and avoid what reality was. I found it hard to draw the line between the past and present and the past became the present!

21

Summary

The past eleven years have been a struggle for me internally and also for my wife and our children. The years since my suicide attempts in 2012 have been a journey of self-discovery, hardship and trying to find the right path for myself and my family to help us move forward. It has by no means been easy, and at times extremely difficult when on occasions I've reached the depths of suicidal thoughts and deep depression. Looking back at the *recent* past I feel that I have robbed myself and my family of a normal and decent life.

Moving forward I have thoughts and aspirations that life will hopefully become better, more meaningful and once again have a purpose to live life to the fullest. These ideas, while being positive are constantly interrupted by the negativity that I face on a day-to-day basis. As a result of my constant need to justify my injury to government agencies every three months, I am always reminded that I have a major illness as a result of my service for my country. Over the years Nancy and I have expended all our energy, in trying to stabilise my health and that of the family rather than having to tackle the complexities of seeking compensation from the NZDF insurer.

As we as a family embark on this next chapter of our lives, we have started the battle of gaining recognition and compensation from the NZDF nominated insurance company. It has been disappointing, to say the least, that during this whole episode I have never been offered compensation by the NZDF, the insurer nor even contacted and advised that this was a path entitled to me as a result of my service. In August 2017 we became aware of the options that should have been open to me in 2012 regarding NZDF insurance and financial support. Being under the care of the NZDF between 2009 – 2016 I should have been told that I was eligible to receive compensation as I had fully met the criteria for Total and Permanent Disability (TPD). The definition of TPD at the time was: "The member has been absent from their usual employment due to sickness or accident for a minimum period of six consecutive months from the date of disablement and is not currently employed elsewhere."[14]

We have been battling through insurance matters with Defence authorities since 2012.

This has been in complete contrast to those veterans who have suffered life changing physical injuries. The separation between physical and mental injuries is still genuine and evident in our society. This is further being hampered by my knowledge of other veterans and individuals who have tried to claim compensation but have been hounded by insurance companies to prove their disabilities and rights. I've heard horrific stories from other sufferers who have been harassed by their insurance companies to the extent of being placed under surveillance both physically and an electronically. The thought of having an organisation overtly intrude into our lives causes immense stress and reluctance to go down the path of seeking compensation. This battle is part of the wider campaign we have started, however, we will continue to be unsure of any outcome well into the future.

---

[14]   Email from the NZDF dated 26 Aug 2017

One of the other major goals of my life moving forward is to ensure the emotional and financial security of my wife and our children. This again seems to be outside of my reach as my many attempts to obtain life insurance and mortgage insurance have been denied. Because of my mental injury and my attempts on my life, I am unable to get life and mortgage insurance because I am deemed too much of a risk, and if I was offered insurance, it would be grossly unaffordable. This is yet another example of my injury being stigmatised to the extent where society keeps reminding me that I am deemed damaged goods and irreparable to the extent where my life has little meaning and usefulness.

Like anybody, as a still relatively young man I have dreams and aspirations for myself and the family, however, these are on hold. One of my goals after completing my PTSD program in Australia was that one day I'd be able to take Nancy and the children on a well-deserved holiday, to thank them for their support and perseverance in my struggle. I also see this as an opportunity to bring our family together again as the children have grown up and moved on with their own lives. It would give us the chance to be together as a family unit enjoying each other's company, mull over the past and even laugh about the good times. Just to be with the family in a setting where we can also talk about the future positively and lovingly.

I constantly feel that I have been pressured by government agencies to return to full-time work and revert to the job market at the same level I was at before 2012. This expectation that my skill set remains unchanged means there is no reason I can't return to the same type of employment. The agencies concerned do not take into account what my aspirations and goals are in the future. I've been told on many occasions by my psychiatrist, clinical psychologist and counsellors that I will *never* return to work that I used to do. This is because being placed back into such environments could cause a relapse and irreparable damage to my health and that of the family. The government agencies refuse to recognise this at all.

To be honest, I don't know where this journey will take me and the family and I are currently not in a position to make such a determination.

I often think about any future employment and whether an employer would take that chance of offering me a job. What company wants an individual who is suffering from PTSD and major depression and who at any stage might succumb to the stresses of the job and be unable to fulfill that role? What happens when these inevitable stresses and triggers occur and my fight and flight instinct takes over, and I have to remove myself from the situation at a moment's notice? Society unwittingly also places pressure on Nancy and me because what they see in brief moments of exposure is a guy who outwardly shows the persona of normality.

What they don't see is the constant internal turmoil that I face on a daily basis, not only as a result of my injury but the normal stresses and strains that are placed on the individual in everyday life.

22

Nancy's Story - Bill the Person

Through reading Bill's story, it is interesting to find what I have actually either blocked out of my mind or how different I find my memories are from Bill's. When I think back to Malaysia, what I do recall is how intoxicated Bill was the first time I saw him after months apart. I had lost a lot of weight and certainly looked quite different, but it wasn't that, because he knew about the weight loss and should have been prepared, after all, I was his wife, and it had only been a few months. I brushed Bill's appearance and behaviour off as him having a blow-out after such a long time in Afghanistan and the lengthy flight. I too was exhausted after a similarly long period travelling from New Zealand (NZ), so thought the first night was a catch-up, sleep night and we both would be totally refreshed in the morning.

I was desperately excited about being able to catch him up on all the happenings from home and what the kids were up to, however, felt I didn't want to bombard him until we had time to relax. When I think back now, a lot of our time together was spent socializing and looking for that next place to sit and relax. However, this meant with alcohol. I have never been a big drinker, so I did feel it took up a lot of quality time and in certain situations, I could only get Bill to communicate and relax enough to talk about what was important to me, if we were in a place that served alcohol. I was always conscious of how difficult it was for Bill to relax, and certainly mindful that Afghanistan was always on his mind; let's face it, the more time we spent together and enjoyed it - the harder it was going to be for him to go back.

Some of the most memorable parts of the holiday were touring the island on motor bikes, shopping for the kids and dining at some amazing places. However, there was always an airy silence when we were in the elevators with women wearing hijabs. If only I knew then what I know now, I would have understood it. PTSD coping mechanisms are significant in hindsight.

I met Bill when I was working at the Australian Defence Intelligence Training Centre in Canungra, on the Gold Coast. He was the Executive Officer at the time and was facing a posting out of the area. Our relationship progressed rather quickly, and before you knew it, we were cleaning out the Army house and on the road to New South Wales. It was hard for me leaving my family on the Gold Coast and equally hard for Bill to leave his two young sons from a previous marriage behind. The new posting never seemed to be a settled period for us and our family, and so Bill decided to leave the Australian Defence Force and pursue a new career path, this just happened to be in NZ. After only eighteen months in Australia, I was not ready to return to NZ, so I asked Bill if we did this, to be fair, for an assurance that we would return to Australia sometime in the future. We agreed on a promised period of eight years, I laugh now, as that was some seventeen years ago. In light of all that has happened in those seventeen years, I can look back and know that things may have seemed a little unfair, but I believe things generally happen for a reason.

It wasn't intended that Bill would re-join the defence forces at any time, after all, we were actually intent on a different career path, but his abilities, connections, and some of our social life's direction back in Christchurch meant that he was soon approached to become part of the NZDF Intelligence Corps, and at the time, it just seemed to work out.

New experiences continued to fill our lives; I spent six months in East Timor as a Senior Corrections Officer for the United Nations and one year later Bill, and I got married on a beach in Australia half way between *his* tour to East Timor. No honeymoon followed; Bill went back to East Timor and I immediately came home to NZ with an unexpected addition to our family. This was when Bill's eldest son at the age of eleven came to live with us. Life as I knew it changed immensely and I continued throughout the next dozen years feeling and operating much like a single parent.

The rest was history, doors opened for him in his field of expertise and, he eventually got posted to HQ JFNZ in Wellington. I stayed behind to pack up the house, sort the kid's schooling, etc. and prepare the house ready to go on the market. Leaving my family and friends again was very difficult for me, but the kids kept me going.

 Life ticked by when Bill was on a tour of duty and he spent many months over a period of four years absent from home. When he left the military, Bill took up jobs that continued to have him constantly away in other places, which I believe made it very difficult for him to fit into family life when he came home. In addition, the kids and I were well into our own routines and carried on as we always did, so when Bill was at home, chaos surrounded us. The over compensating by Bill, possibly out of guilt for being absent so much, coupled with my stickler for routines and normality where the kids were concerned, definitely clashed big time. The kids played us off against each other, to the point that Bill and I viewed most things differently. However, I could not understand why he would fly off the handle at things I thought were minute and then the opposite, things that I thought were important, were uninteresting to him.

This went on for years, and it felt like a stranger was living with me – my husband at home in body but not really there, if that makes sense? - In his own world.

23

Reflections

Today I find myself thinking about things that on the one hand appear extremely confusing and on the other hand, make absolute sense. When Bill asked me to add my part in this story I felt really angry with the thought of having to re-live a lot of emotions, thoughts and events that I have worked so hard, in the last half dozen years to block out from my mind. Being faced with this book, and being asked to add my perspective felt like such a daunting task, and one more part of this interminable journey I have been on with Bill. Don't get me wrong, I love my husband very much and there have also been many extraordinary good times, but PTSD has become such a dominant feature in our lives for so long, that it's easy to feel completed swallowed up by it.

There are times I felt extremely angry, and that anger came from a place where life revolved around Bill, his PTSD and its related consequences. Where I would have to continually not only look after myself but take care of the kids and their emotions too. I was also in full protection mode over a lot of things he would say and do. Today I would love to know how Bill's actions were perceived by the kids; how they felt back then and to see if they were probably just as angry as I was. As I said previously we were married in Australia, during his tour of East Timor and within a couple of days he went back to East Timor and I was heading home back home to NZ with an eleven-year-old stepson. That in itself was probably the start of where my life changed so much, and I don't think I was quite prepared.

I think I was harbouring resentment a little even before Bill's tour to Afghanistan started. We were living in Christchurch at the time, and there were the normal difficult challenges and adjustments to get through as all blended families experience. Whilst I had the support of family and friends, the only person I wanted to talk to was Bill. However, it was not long before Bill would say that every time he rang home from overseas, it was very difficult for him to hear of any problems arising at home. I understood his focus had to be on his job overseas and although he couldn't fix any issues arising at home, I just wanted to keep him involved. This is possibly where a little resentment came from, because he certainly couldn't do what he was doing without my support and it wasn't feeling like a two-way street. This became a repeating pattern over the years. All of a sudden our lives were exciting one minute with new beginnings, but then the novelties wore off pretty quickly.

I knew a lot of people in similar circumstances where the partners were at home trying to keep things as normal as possible but I'd done a tour, and I knew how difficult it was. So I just carried on, and I think in part, the more time Bill spent away, the more the distance grew between him and his family. We did work out at one stage that Bill had been away for approximately four years in total, at times when our kids were going through the typical teens. Bill was absent for most of this time instead of being there for which were really crucial times, I believe in a teenager's life. Fortunately, the kids appeared fairly resilient but the relationship they had with their dad through those years changed.

As they grew older they stood up to their father, but Bill's anger was something we all could not understand. I was an adult and could handle it, but the kids? I just wanted to protect them and keep them out of the line of fire from the unwarranted, angry outbursts their father would display. We carried on as we had done routinely without Bill around, but that also seemed to have formed a resentment within him. I credit the kids as my saviour during some upsetting times, and am so grateful for their love and support. I struggled with Bill's anger which, over a number of years increased in intensity with unexpected and unpredictable behaviour.

On his return from Afghanistan, Bill was certainly not the person I had married before he left.

I had come to expect unpredictable behaviour from him but nothing this dramatic. It seemed like there was no turning back for him. I remember spending so much time trying to explain to the kids that dad is not himself and nothing was their fault. I felt I was constantly trying to explain something which actually I didn't understand myself..... Our lives turned upside down for what? Why? What had *we* done?

Several years on, I know now it was not us, but like me, the kids were hurting too and didn't understand why he was so angry at everything all the time.

We literally walked on eggshells, however there were times we stood up to him and told him how we were feeling, struggling with the love we had for him, wishing everything could be normal.

I think I always knew I would support Bill and help him to rebuild family relationships during what we described as some 'toxic' times, provided he wanted to help himself. I know he harbours deep regrets for putting us through those challenges, something he didn't understand himself at the time.

So another new journey began; we moved house again and I continued to support Bill for I knew he was still a good man, however more often than not, he wasn't a *nice* person.

Bill's youngest son would come on holidays, and he also knew that things were not always right with his dad. Bill had a short fuse and boys being boys would push buttons that I think they both wish they hadn't.

At some point, I always thought that if Bill were prepared to help himself, then I would be there to help. Also if he'd continue to go down the destructive path he was on and was not prepared to accept help, then I don't think we would be on this journey together. I certainly wouldn't be writing about things today, so with that said I decided that I needed to seek some assistance from wherever I could get it. Initially, I thought that Bill displayed all the signs and symptoms of a male mid-life crisis, and that he was going get through whatever this was, and we would just carry on. I think back now, and maybe I was really just looking for a label, somewhere to start to put the behaviours into context - I guess.

It became quite clear that Bill was unsettled in general, taking up high profile positions, travelling, not happy, etc. I struggled with his destructive patterns of behaviour, struggling with normality, constantly sheltering the kids from his unpredictability. This life consumed me, to the point I isolated myself from others and found little enjoyment with anything I did, unless I was close to the kids.

After Bill's first suicide attempt, I was in shock. I saw him as selfish, and immediately kicked into the parent protective mode. I was still a wife and mother but struggled with my emotions, as I could not see anything else past what he had done and the situation that he had created for all of us. Throughout his recovery, there were many times where I just wanted to walk away; I had to keep a close eye on him 24/7, and I was exhausted. I came to realize that this was not about me because I can make my own choices. I had worked so hard over the years to block out a lot of the PTSD consequences out and it's been rather a difficult task to recall my thoughts from those dark times.

24

Coping After Suicide

When do you ever prepare yourself in life to help cut your husband down or any family member for that matter, after an attempt to hang themselves? I do remember multiple doctors diagnosing Bill's depression and the constant reminder of a deep wound around his neck from the rope, but more than anything, I remember the 'label'. Finally things started making sense, depression, avoidance, a diagnosis until finally everything became clear. This was absolutely nothing to do with me or his family. This was a battle he was fighting from within and we were *all* fighting it together.

Once PTSD was finally out in the open, I could start doing my own research. However, it did just come down to a label. The consequences of depression were only one of the many signs of his diagnosed chronic PTSD, all as a result of the traumatic events stemming from his tour of Afghanistan. Bill's actions over the last few years cut way deeper than just having a label. Saying it out loud didn't make all the bad stuff go away, and the kids would often say to me "Mum it's not an excuse and you don't have to accept inappropriate behaviour". They were right of course, but after a while, even though it's pretty sad, I hadn't realised that I actually had come to accept his behaviour as normal and routine.

So in a matter of six weeks, in addition to being a full-time mother and in full-time employment, I had a very sick husband who had made two attempts to end his life. I remember saying to myself in an exhausted state "I don't think I can stay awake anymore to watch him 24 hours a day." He had some medication for depression and was attending some medical appointments but if he really wanted to go down that path, I may not be able to stop him. The situation scared me, but I really had to accept that as well. A lot of the details of those months are a blur now. Fortunately, I did learn quickly how good a liar Bill had become around avoidance and what he wanted the doctors to hear.

"Crikey!" I thought, "what on earth was going to make *me* equipped to deal with him in such a mental state?"

I have vivid memories of going to a part of the hospital where they locked Bill in a room and removed his shoe laces and belt. He looked at me through the little window in the door, and the guilt ran through me. This was not dissimilar to the familiar surroundings of my previous employment, working in a prison. It was really like the movies, getting locked up in a mental institution or a prison facility. I remember driving home from the hospital that night thinking, "If they release him tomorrow what does that mean; is he a danger to himself, to the kids or is it something that's going to affect the rest of our lives if he continues down this path?" I could not bear the thought of the kids finding him in such a state as I had found him previously after his suicide attempts. I do remember though, that for the first time in a long time, thinking I was going to be able to get a good night's sleep, knowing he was under observation and would be safe.

⊢———⊣

I was woken the next day by a phone call from Bill to say that I could go and pick him up. My initial thought was shock: "How can I look after him? I can't watch him all the time". When I arrived at the hospital, I found the meeting with Bill and the professionals had already started without me. Bill was spinning some good yarns and talking the talk, convincing the doctors that everything was okay. I was confused at this; the suicide attempts were being passed off as something that was a temporary lapse and he was going to be much better with a few pills.

Despite my shock and protestations, Bill was released for home - after all, he had nowhere else to go. I don't think I slept more than a couple of hours for days due to that constant fear of the unknown. There was sleep deprivation, anxiety and a multitude of emotions that I was continually battling with. The kids stayed with friends, whose parents understood to a certain degree but given the stigma of suicide as a selfish act, I didn't say too much. I put on a very brave face day after day and would have a smile on my face for the times I had to. Only to collapse between those hours and just coping as a protective parent!

Bill, on the other hand, continued to battle every day. It took a while for me to accept it, but this time he really was totally committed to turning things around for himself, for us!

I took him to multiple appointments with psychiatrists, doctors, and professionals, all offering advice, not only to him but to me also. I would generally get the line "Nancy, you need to have a break too". What this meant at the time I had no idea. That in itself would frustrate me because the practical aspects of my own care were just totally beyond comprehension. That would mean leaving him at home by himself, or with the kids for that matter. I certainly could not be happy anywhere else with the constant worry of Bill being alone and the lack of trust I had in him.

Bill often refers to a turning point in his life when our daughter and I were at his hospital bed, after his overdose. This was something we had done after his first attempt, but for some reason, this time something had clicked inside of him. Once he had decided that he needed help, rather than avoiding and pretending like he was in control of his life, things started to change. It was at that point that I really believed if he wanted to make that change, I would support him to achieve it. Over these last few years however nothing has stopped me from looking over my shoulder and continually being in a state of anxiousness.

Whilst minimal now, there are still days and moments in time that choke you, and send you right back into that dark space. I have spent the best part of the last six years trying to work my way through this journey of support. I have grown a lot along the way; have a better understanding of PTSD, and have supported Bill in his advocacy at the many events he has been invited to as a guest speaker. By doing this, I have the utmost compassion for the many PTSD sufferers and their families. Raising PTSD awareness is important to us both as it seems to come to light more and more every day. Our journey specifically relates to veterans, but we all know that there are many sufferers of PTSD, for example, survivors of the devastating Christchurch earthquakes, or the many emergency service volunteers, who on a daily basis deal with many traumatic events and then just everyday New Zealanders that are vulnerable to such symptoms.

25

The Invictus Games

I want to acknowledge one part of our journey that although it has many lows and stable moments, there were also some of the best highs that came with being a PTSD supporter, such as, attending the inaugural 2014 Invictus Games, initiated by Prince Henry (or Prince Harry as the world knows him). This was also a time through Bill's journey when I remember his anxiety being heightened to limits beyond imagination. Bill was there to represent NZ in the relay event and had trained for it as part of his PTSD recovery.

It was a journey within a journey. As we left Wellington for Auckland and then on to Singapore with the last leg to London where the games were being held. Four hundred competitors and a handful of support people for those who needed that close assistance- all staying in the St Pauls Hotel, London.

We arrived in London and wouldn't you know it, the airline forgot to put our bags on the plane from Wellington. You can imagine how this went down. Bill had no uniforms, no formal function attire and the bulk of the much needed medications to see him through. Basically, what we had with us in our carry-on luggage was it. We were given £100 pounds and sent on our way to await the process of luggage recovery.

Having no luggage normally is enough to set any sane person into a spin, let alone someone coping with chronic PTSD and anxiety. On the inside I was fuming at the thought of having no toiletries, underwear or spare clothes, but on the outside, I had to remain the total calming package for Bill and support him through his extremely raised anxiety.

The next couple of days were spent trying to find some clothes, shoes, socks etc for Bill to wear at the upcoming formal function at the NZ High Commission in London. It was fantastic catching up with a familiar face in Brigadier Lofty Hayward, who held the appointment of Defence Attaché to the UK and was instrumental in Prince Harry's attendance to meet with the Kiwi (New Zealand) Invictus team. In our acquired temporary attire, both Bill and I were not feeling that comfortable but I encouraged Bill to try and enjoy himself while I continued to liaise with the airline about getting our luggage to London.

After an amazing opening ceremony the assembled athletes were addressed by the Royal Family, the games' events began. At the end of that first day, we went back to the hotel to relax with other competitors. I think this was the first time I had witnessed Bill laugh, and I mean actually laugh. He was finally surrounded by people from around the world with similar diagnosis and PTSD symptoms. They could take the 'mickey' out of each other and get away with it and understand each other's pain without going into details. This was magical to see. As a support person, I too could sit there with the partner of one of our Swiss friends and 'chew the fat' or chat about anything and everything. We found we could laugh at common things and vent at the sacrifices PTSD has demanded of us and our families without judgement.

We were one of the luckiest of many countries at the games to have the honour of our VC (Victoria Cross) Corporal Willie Apiata being with us as our patron. Willie has received his VC as a result of his actions under fire in Afghanistan in 2004. During this trip, I personally spent a lot of time with Willie. His presence was a pure inspiration to our small NZ team and this showed on the many occasions he joined in and led the team prior to events. It didn't take long to realize that we were envied by other countries for his presence, to the point we all felt a little stalked for that one and only photo opportunity, but his loyalty was always to the team first. I remember so well the pride of being a Kiwi when he led us all in an amazing, inspirational HAKA (our traditional Maori war cry) that was enjoyed by a packed stadium, prior to a wheel chair rugby match between NZ and the UK.

Other highlights included Willie and me getting Bill through one of his worst anxiety moments, which presented during an event. Ten minutes before the NZ swim relay team of which Bill was a member, were about to start their race, I could see Bill with a look of absolute fear on his face. I had seen this look previously on the plane when Bill knew he couldn't control an exit route during mid-flight. Obviously, we are here today to tell the story, so he breathed through it, but prior to this swim race, breathing exercises simply were not going to cut it. This wasn't just about him not wanting to swim in the centre lane, this was about the anxiety and fear of being stuck in the middle lane and not being able to get out, he needed to be near the edge. Willie and I certainly had to put our military caps on and get to work to resolve the issue. We went behind the scenes to the organizers who were adamant that it was too late to change lanes and the NZ team would need to be pulled from the race if all four competitors could not swim. *"Oh yay, more pressure for Bill to deal with."* I remember seeing and talking to everybody we could talk to in such a short space of time before they announced our withdrawal. I knew this would only *heighten* his anxiety if that was possible, Bill's sense of failure and letting others down would devastate him. We found the top dog and explained the situation in such a way that pulling the team would do nothing for what Invictus stood for. We did it, I remember that awesome but painful high five with Willie over our accomplishment.

The Invictus games certainly tested and tried my supporter status on many levels, however mixing with such awesome people, first and foremast an amazing NZ team with their extraordinary strength and courage. And the royals and celebrities who displayed compassion and understanding; our VC Willie Apiata, with whom I had many laughs as he helped keep me sane. They are all just amazing human beings who have used their status in life to support the wounded warriors to live again.

Towards the end of the games, I had the fortune to hang out in the hotel with one on the competitors from the USA. She told me something that night that has forever rung in my ears. This beautiful young lady lost both her legs (right up to the hips) as a result of an Improvised Explosive Device (IED) in Afghanistan. We started talking about hers and Bill's injuries and she told me that she was the lucky one. This really puzzled me, but please understand I by no means compare her situation with any other sufferer and their pain journey. So I asked her, what do you mean by that and she said..... *"Well, I lost my legs and although I went through a few years of phantom pain, I now have that under control and am sporting these fantastic titanium legs that I have grown to love. My physical injury has been surgically dealt with and I am relatively pain free. I have been able to achieve so much under the circumstances and can move on with my life"*. She went on to further add that *"I have a friend in a very similar situation to Bill's, in that he has a mental injury and it just can't be treated like my physical one"*.

After so many years, I now understand what she was talking about. There is no quick fix for PTSD, no surgery, no proposed healing date, no one medication to make it all normal, just a never-ending journey that no one can write the ending for.

I came home from London revived and it was probably the first time I really knew what it meant by the words 'YOU ARE NOT ALONE'.

My journey as a PTSD supporter continues, and a part of me feels I really want this to be behind me so I can continue on in some form of normality. Life has changed, Bill is not the person I married fifteen years ago but he is a new person with different outlooks. Change can be great with forgiveness, love and compassion. I have three amazing children in my life to whom I credit my sanity over the years and can now relish in the control I have back of my own life. I look back over the last year where I have been able to travel, especially internationally with sport again, something I dearly missed over the last seven years. Bill accompanies me at times and gets himself involved. However, I have learned to accept that he can only do what he feels good about doing and when he wants to do it. I have come to accept that while it may not always fair, it's part my new life and that's ok. He surprises me in good and bad ways, with glimpses of the old Bill, but they keep everything going forward - a nice gesture just puts everything else into insignificance. This is where I seem to forget about the PTSD journey and smile as I get reminded of my new normality. I think we will always continue to work towards that balance. My life has changed so much, and I am often checking myself at a new level of personal contentment. This was not how I envisaged my life to turn out, but I have grown, and I think it's okay as a support person to say to a sufferer "This is what I am doing and it's up to you whether you join me".

26

The Journey Continues

As I sat in the room in Sydney, I find myself pondering thoughts of a little trepidation and some excitement. We had just completed the final visit to Richmond Hospital, and I must admit there was a little bit of anxiety shown by both of us. I wasn't too sure how Bill would feel knowing that the treatment program was coming to an end. I could certainly understand his apprehension.

I feel I took something very powerful and positive away from our last visit that came from the little exercise that we were asked to do. As a couple we were asked to look at five simple questions over three separate areas as follows:

The five questions related to:

1. How you are spending your time?
2. What took your energy?
3. What has changed?
4. What are you most proud of?
5. What would you like to change?

The three areas were:

1. One year ago,

2. A current life,

3. One year from now.

This process seemed quite simple, but I was really surprised at how well connected both Bill and I were when answering the questions. If we look at one year ago Bill described himself as disengaged from family and home life, his memory was non-existent, we were fighting compensation issues, we were media focused to attend this treatment program in Australia and I was an advocate for all of Bill's PTSD matters.

Moving on to the current life, again we both seemed to be on the same page. We agreed that Bill was more engaged with family, he would cook meals and could organise things such as a warrant of fitness for the car or dog registrations, and even appointments to meet deadlines. He could even concentrate long enough to build me a beautiful swing seat of which he knew was always something I dreamed of. It was one of the best birthday presents he has ever given me, partly because of the thought and physical effort that had gone into it, but a lot to do with how proud he was of himself for his achievement. We agreed that his short-term memory is better and that we have sorted some of the beneficiary compensation issues and is now moving on to a further claim for which he may be entitled to. Other achievements include this book, a renewed focus on the here and now and what's important, more activities done around the home, little things that he couldn't do before. He is more in control of his future, and is partly able to communicate with professionals without my having to be the 100% advocate for him. Bill now has hearing aids and while he might not use them all the time, they have also certainly improved communications!

This brings us to where we would like to be a year from now. It includes, but is certainly not limited to:

4. A secure future with less PTSD worries,

5. A successfully published book,

6. A better understanding and closer family unit,

and of course, with a little humour, obviously winning lotto and having Bill finish building the kitchen table would be a huge bonus.

Completing the program has given us the tools on both our belts to move forward and plan a future. Bill would like his future to be productive and to keep himself occupied but at this stage has no idea what that is, given his PTSD symptoms will almost indefinitely prevent him from the normality he once knew.

On the 19 July 2017, we walked 8 km from Coogee to Bondi Beach in Sydney, Australia. Both of us being unwell with a nasty cold and cough. It was such a pleasure to be outside finally in sunshine although the wind was cold. It was the first time I think I have ever told Bill about the personal cost of PTSD and what that toll has had on me. The sacrifices, the tears and the general loss of personal enjoyment that I had lost. I was finally able to explain to him that for the last six years I feel like I have just been marking time and everything has revolved around PTSD. This was a huge milestone, because I felt I could talk from the heart, and it was not said to hurt Bill but because he now can understand the sacrifices his family have made. And again for the first time ever, we didn't dwell on what we have lost but focused on what we would like and where we would like to be a year from now.

It was a deep and very real conversation, with some dreams, some realities and some potential positive possibilities. Life will be lived with PTSD, but I don't think it will continue to be *controlled* by PTSD. I do believe there is a jagged road ahead, even never ending, but it's a road I don't mind travelling. I have a smile on my face as I think back to that walk. Bill told me what to do, in particular where I should sit. I just looked at him, smiled and said: *"You are kidding me, you are telling me where to sit?"*

He looked at me for a long moment and didn't say another word. This is huge because he recognizes this is progress. So I guess PTSD will always be with us, where in every situation he will still feel he needs to be in control. The exit points will still need to be covered for any quick escape and safety procedures will still need to be in place for his peace of mind. I now have the confidence to say to him that it's okay, we are ok and can make our own decisions.

In the past to keep the peace, it would have been easier to just sit in that spot to make him feel better, but knowing what I know now, it's not necessary. I am allowed to challenge him, and I think slowly but surely, I can teach him that trying to control every situation does not necessarily make it safe and others can voice that as well. I have learnt that I can be a support person, but I also can live my own life and take back that control of myself. I can do this and still show compassion and support while at the same time live and rejuvenate. I finally have that courage to stand up for what is right in any particular moment and challenge if necessary what is acceptable without the dramatic consequences that PTSD can present.

⊢———⊣

Abbreviations

ACC –New Zealand Crown .The entity responsible for administering the country's universal no-fault accidental injury scheme.

ANA - Afghan Nation Army The new Afghan National Army was founded with the issue of a decree by President Hamid Karzai on December 1, 2002

CFC – A Combined Forces Command – Afghanistan

CI - Counter-Intelligence. Information gathered and activities conducted to identify, deceive, exploit, disrupt, or protect against espionage, other intelligence activities, sabotage, or assassinations conducted for or on behalf of foreign powers, organizations or persons or their agents, or international terrorist organizations or activities. Also called CI. See also counterespionage; security. (JP 2-01.2)[15]

CIA - Central Intelligence Agency

CJTF-76 - Combined Joint Task Force 180/76 Essentially a divisional size HQ responsible for several tasks around the country, based on an effective vision out of CFC-A

---

[15]   2017 http://www.dtic.mil/doctrine/new_pubs/dictionary.pdf

COIN - Comprehensive civilian and military efforts designed to simultaneously defeat and contain insurgency and address its root causes. (JP 3-24)[16]

DEA – (USA) Drug Enforcement Agency

HESCO Bastions - Collapsible wire mesh containers with a heavy duty lining filled with sand, soil or gravel that forms a temporary to semi-permanent levee or blast wall against explosions or small-arms.

HQJFNZ–Headquarters Joint Forces New Zealand was established at Trentham on 01 July 2001 to support the Commander of Joint Forces New Zealand in his command of assigned forces. These forces essentially include all deployable NZDF Force Elements.[17]

HUMINT - Human Intelligence. A category of intelligence derived from information collected and provided by human sources. (JP 2-0)[18]

HVT – High Value Target. A target the enemy commander requires for the successful completion of the mission. (JP 3-60)[19] The loss of high-value targets would be expected to seriously degrade important enemy functions. E.g. Osama bin Laden.

IFC - Intelligence Fusion Cell which dealt with the regional analysis of day-to-day intelligence support for operations.

J-2X Staff - The staff element of the intelligence directorate of a joint staff that combines and represents the principal authority for counterintelligence and human intelligence support. (JP 2-01.2)[20]

NGO – Non-Government Organisation

NZDF – New Zealand Defence Force

---

[16]   2017 http://www.dtic.mil/doctrine/new_pubs/dictionary.pdf

[17]   2017 http://www.nzdf.mil.nz/about-us/hqjfnz/default.htm

[18]   2017 http://www.dtic.mil/doctrine/new_pubs/dictionary.pdf

[19]   2017 http://www.dtic.mil/doctrine/new_pubs/dictionary.pdf

[20]   2017 http://www.dtic.mil/doctrine/new_pubs/jp2_01.pdf

OFC - Other Coalition Forces Were in charge of unconventional forces and tier one targeting known as black operations.

PRT - Provincial Reconstruction Team. PRTs in Afghanistan are key instruments through which the international community delivers assistance at the provincial and district level. As a result of their provincial focus and civilian and military resources, PRTs have a unique mandate to improve security, support good governance, and enhance provincial development. The combination of international civilian and military resources also allows the PRT to have wide latitude to implement their mandate.[21]

SAG - Security Analysis Group. This forum comprised representatives from all organisations with security interests in Afghanistan. The formation of the group had a significant impact on improving information sharing and on situational awareness, as well as in operational planning and the subsequent execution of a wide variety of counterinsurgency activity, both kinetic, and in reconstruction and development.

SCIF (pronounced "skiff) - Sensitive Compartmented Information Facility. An accredited area, room, group of rooms, or installation where sensitive compartmented information may be stored, used, discussed, and/or electronically processed. Where procedural and physical measures prevent the free access of persons unless they have been formally indoctrinated for the particular sensitive compartmented information authorized for use or storage within the sensitive compartmented information facility.[22]

---

[21]   2017 https://www.usaid.gov/provincial-reconstruction-teams

[22]   2017 http://www.dtic.mil/doctrine/new_pubs/dictionary.pdf

SNO - Senior National Officer. Responsible for all New Zealand troops posted within the Kabul area of operations. These included officers who were posted to the International Security Assistance Force (ISAF), New Zealand Army trainers and other staff within the Kabul region.

UNAMA - United Nations Assistance Mission in Afghanistan

Whilst this is Willie and myself helping Jason get back to the other end of the pool, to me this is a reminder of how much in awe we were of the strength and courage shown by our wounded warrior competitors. The team were my heroes.

Another event at the games was a celebrity rugby match where Individuals from each country were selected to participate. This was an awesome moment for both Bill and me. I took this photo which highlights what the games were about, where royalty, celebrities and competitors from around the world could have a great banter and just be themselves. Prince Harry turned up on his pushbike, and turned away paparazzi requests for

moments like this. Just prior to this photo, Bill and Harry were both waiting for a ball pass from their respective team mates and collided in their competitiveness. I do remember saying to myself "It's not every day you can watch your husband go head to head with a royal family member." I will never forget the fun everybody had and the priceless moments in the green room with other celebrities like Johnny Wilkinson, Sir Clive Woodward, Mike Robinson, Zara Phillips, Mike Tindal etc. At the end of the day we are all just human and fun was had by all, including Willie who wanted to join in on the fun and injuries were momentarily forgotten.

Acknowledgements

A special thanks to my friend, classmate and brother in arms, Hamish Shearer who brought me out of my shell and enabled me to believe in myself and confront the past without the feeling of shame.

To the staff of St John of God Hospital in North Richmond, Sydney, Australia and especially my fellow course mates with whom I couldn't have faced the daunting task of completing this book. Our special bond is one that will last a life time – thank you for your support, honesty and friendship.

A special thankyou to my phycologist, Jane, who has been there for Nancy and me over the last 10 years, especially in the times when things were not so rosy. Your support and guidance and counselling have been the mainstay of my continued recovery.

I would like to acknowledge the dedication and persistence of my beta readers Tracey Topp, Karina Andrew and Jo Hassan.

Finally, to these special people who have made this all a reality, Pop Maxwell, Marty Donoghue and all our friends who have supported us through this journey.

In addition, this book could not have become a reality without the support of all those individuals and organisations who have contributed to making this a reality.

Finally, to my publishing coach Dixie Maria Carlton with your constant guidance and belief in my journey I was able to finally write and complete this book which has been in the making for the last four years.

I would also especially like to thank Kevin K. Frank, PhD, CAPTAIN, US Navy (ret) for trust he had in my abilities and vision in building our Intelligence Directorate in Afghanistan; his mentoring and for his ongoing support and encouragement through this journey.

www.ingramcontent.com/pod-product-compliance
Lightning Source LLC
Chambersburg PA
CBHW070444090426
42735CB00012B/2454